GOD'S MIGHTY ARMIES
AND HIS GREEN BERETS

RUTH LEE

WestBow
PRESS
A DIVISION OF THOMAS NELSON

WestBow Press books may be ordered through booksellers or by contacting:

WestBow Press
A Division of Thomas Nelson
1663 Liberty Drive
Bloomington, IN 47403
www.westbowpress.com
1-(866) 928-1240

Because of the dynamic nature of the Internet, any web addresses or links contained in this book may have changed since publication and may no longer be valid. The views expressed in this work are solely those of the author and do not necessarily reflect the views of the publisher, and the publisher hereby disclaims any responsibility for them.

Any people depicted in stock imagery provided by Thinkstock are models, and such images are being used for illustrative purposes only.

Certain stock imagery © Thinkstock.

ISBN: 978-1-4497-5760-1 (sc)
ISBN: 978-1-4497-5759-5 (e)

Library of Congress Control Number: 2012911277

Printed in the United States of America

WestBow Press rev. date: 08/08/2012

CONTENTS

INTRODUCTION

Throughout life, many strive to become the men and women God wants them to be. Progress seems slow, and they see little change in their lives. Then one day a situation calling for faith and action arises, and they find themselves responding, unaware that they are acting beyond their abilities. A response requires years of study and prayer during life's struggles.

To become a warrior takes much training. It can mean years of working to be strong in the Lord and gain the ability and willingness to fight for your beliefs and free others from the onslaught of Satan. This process begins shortly after your commitment to God. Unaware of what is taking place, some view life as merely a series of problems and experiences. Later, it becomes clear what God is doing through life's many trials. A soldier spends much time in training before he enters battle; David had a great deal of training before taking out Goliath. A mighty man of valor must not become discouraged or quit while in training.

In this book, I offer many examples of how you are to surrender all for the kingdom and be willing to rely on God's plans for your spiritual lives. You must give up many things to do what God has planned for you.

I challenge you to be willing to let God take you to heights and depths that seem impossible without Him. Trust Him to keep you strong during your training to fight demons.

There are times when we cannot comprehend the ways of our Lord. Often this is God's way of preparing us to reach another level. You can be a dynamic Christian, an intercessor, one whose life is pure before God; you can be a worshiper in the spirit and ascend to glorious heights in Him. Yet something is drawing you to seek more of His excellence. You do everything you know. Still your prayers cannot gain what you desire. That is when you need Special Forces, and perhaps God desires you to join them.

What are the Special Forces? An army unit may be doing a good job in battle, but sometimes it is not properly equipped or cannot leave its position to take on pockets of the enemy set up and camouflaged to catch soldiers off guard. But the Special Forces have been alerted, perhaps by a reconnaissance plane sent to search out dangers or by intelligence officers who have overheard enemy plans. The military will then send in the Green Berets to take out the enemy positions so the regular army can advance without hindrance. Applying this to our spiritual battles, those who are capable of spiritual warfare can be called in to clear out pockets of demonic powers assigned by Satan to hinder the work of the church, a family, or an individual. Pastors especially need these strong Christians whom God has prepared for such warfare. If this is what you need, my book will be a help to you. You will see people with different callings, abilities, and missions, and how they have been trained.

In examining the organization of God's kingdom, we discover that He has those who pray, praise, and worship calling on Him. Yet another group carries out God's plans so people will have a proper place to worship. Some have more than one duty. One group cannot function properly without the other.

Pastors need all these ministries to carry out their work as leaders. Relying on them does not detract from their authority or leadership. God has a plan for success, and if all the faithful stand in their own place and calling, the church can storm the gates of hell. Step by step, we progress toward this goal.

CHAPTER 1

BOOT CAMP, FOXHOLES, AND WEAPONS

Military stories are the foundation for this book. Focusing on stories about our troops recalls the way Jesus used natural things to explain the spiritual in his teachings. Knowing these stories made His messages more understandable to listeners. Green Berets are known as the deadliest warriors and are the main subject of this book. I begin with the army because that is the branch of service in which you will find the Green Berets.

The US Army, Air Force, Navy, and Marine Corps safeguard the air, land, and sea. God is also putting together a mighty army of prayer warriors, workers, preachers, teachers, and other combat forces to fight spiritual enemies and liberate the oppressed. As I equate this army with the armies of this world, I hope to offer a greater understanding of God's mighty armies and His Green Berets. There is great comfort in knowing that a well-qualified military force is always alert to the dangers lurking around us. As we observe these well-trained military forces, we feel more secure in a world full of turmoil.

The army was the first branch of the armed services established by Congress. The US Army evolved from the Continental army, which was created on July 14, 1775, by the Continental Congress to fight the Revolutionary War.

The United States Army Special Forces, also known as the Green Berets because of their distinctive service headgear, are a special operations force tasked with six primary missions: unconventional warfare, foreign internal defense, special reconnaissance, direct action, hostage rescue, and counterterrorism. The first two emphasize language, cultural, and training skills in working with foreign troops. Other duties include combat search and rescue, security assistance, peacekeeping, humanitarian assistance, counter-proliferation, psychological operations, manhunts, and counter-drug operations. Other components of the United States Special Operational Command and other US government agencies may also specialize in these secondary areas.

The Green Berets' official motto, "To liberate the oppressed," could well apply to God's army. One of the Green Berets' primary missions is training and advising foreign indigenous forces. Your most powerful weapon is your mind. If you possess boundless ideas and creativity and always imagine new ways to organize and strategize, the army wants to talk to you. Today's warfare has new rules and calls for a different type of soldier. You need to be mentally superior, creative, highly trained, and physically tough. Alone or as part of a team, you'll work in diverse conditions, act as a diplomat, and get the job done in hostile situations. You may have to live in a foreign country for months. Green Berets are the army's most specialized experts in unconventional warfare.

To become part of the Special Forces, you must endure difficult training and face all challenges head-on. Special Forces soldiers are either on a real-world mission or training for one. Their missions are conducted worldwide and are sometimes classified. They range from stopping acts of terrorism to supporting the global war on terror to aiding humanitarian efforts.

The navy traces its origins to 1775 and the American Revolution. A fleet established to fight the British was disbanded after the war, but the need for a naval force was again recognized in 1798 when Congress established the Department of the Navy. The navy was a separate government department until the National Security Act of 1947 created the Department of Defense, with a cabinet-level secretary to oversee all branches of the military.

The Aeronautical Division of the Army Signal Corps, the precursor to the US Air Force, was established on August 1, 1907. The First Aero Squadron was organized in 1914 and served with the Mexican Border Expedition in 1916. The air force remained a division of the army until 1947. The air force is responsible for domestic security in such areas as deterring air and missile attacks and conducting space surveillance. Other responsibilities of the air force include maintaining a combat-ready mobile strike force and operating air bases in key areas around the world.

Steeped in history, tradition, and folklore, the Marine Corps, a self-contained amphibious combat force within the Department of the Navy, traces its roots to the Revolutionary War. During its two-hundred-year history, the Marine Corps has fulfilled its obligation to provide air, land, and sea support for naval forces, establish beachheads during war, and protect US lives and interests at foreign embassies and legations. The marines maintain a large reserve unit that, when mobilized in times of crisis, can increase the corps' strength by 25 percent within weeks.

The US Coast Guard was first established in 1790 as the US Revenue Cutter Service under the Department of the Treasury. It later moved to the Department of Transportation, where it remained for thirty-six years. On February 25, 2003, the coast guard was transferred to the Department of Homeland Security, comprising about one-fourth of the new department's budget. The coast guard is charged with protecting the country's coasts against smuggling, enforcing customs laws, and responding to coastal emergencies. The move to the Department of Homeland Security did not change the coast guard's mission significantly, although it is now responsible for securing the nation's ports and is prepared to take part in international conflicts in the war on terrorism.

Our armed forces are not enough. As powerful as they are, even with meticulous planning, well-trained forces, and our state-of-the-art artillery, they could never eliminate the least angel of hell. But our military must be ready when Satan sends out these angelic beings to inspire leaders of other countries to make war on us and other nations and try to defeat our armies. We need our troops to be well prepared and our Special Forces to be ever on guard. It is even more important for the armies of God to be ever ready to combat the spiritual forces that plot against our nation. Prayer has won more battles than we could ever imagine. When we pray for our leaders, God can give them a plan to defend our nation.

CHAPTER 2

OLD TESTAMENT ARMIES

God's hand has rested on armies throughout history, beginning with the Old Testament era. At all times, his faithfulness remains the same.

God has always had a people who were prepared to take on the enemy. We find many examples of specially trained forces in the Old Testament. They were ordinary people who submitted to God and learned the ways of heavenly warfare. Perhaps they were tired of the way the kingdom of God was being hindered by Satan. We learn about these special agents by reading what is recorded in God's textbook and following the example of the old patriarchs.

We can see in Scripture how God used men and women. We see how God took David at a young age and began his training while he went about his everyday duties. Though these may seem small to us, I am sure the bear he faced was perplexing and the lion was no small matter. He had no one to call for help when one of these beasts attacked his sheep. He had to face them alone. Most likely he had spent time in prayer and had learned to depend on God to help him to destroy his enemies. Were it not for these dangers and victories, David would not have been prepared to face the giant, a special assignment. The armies at hand were not involved in that battle.

David was a member of God's Special Forces. Like a Green Beret, he was well trained and well assured that he could do what needed to be done. We do not know the hours David put into practice with his sling before he was accurate enough to kill a giant, nor what method he used to strengthen his body. But could it be that he not only kept watch over the sheep but also was most likely carrying wounded sheep, pulling them out of pits or embankments, and wrestling wild animals that got too near the fold? (And all the while, he was becoming skilled on the harp.) The training he received could not be accomplished in the city or at his home; he had to be placed in a certain environment with just the right kind of responsibilities, situations, and dangers that would prepare him to be both a warrior and a special agent.

People like David are very seldom famous. Usually they are just common people. David was the least thought of in his family and the least likely to become anything important, but God does not judge by outward appearance. He sees what we cannot. David was not only a slayer of the giant; he also trained other men how to war against the strongest opposition. When he was old, others stood ready to take the challenge. Not all his men were capable of this type of fighting, but some had the courage to face anything.

In the first book of Samuel, we learn that at first David had to endure the ridicule of his older brothers for even being at the scene of his battle with Goliath: "And Eliab his eldest brother heard when he spake unto the men; and Eliab's anger was kindled against David, and he said, Why camest thou down hither? And with whom hast thou left those few sheep in the wilderness? I know thy pride, and the naughtiness of thine heart; for thou art come down that thou mightiest see the battle. And David said, what have I now done? Is there not a cause?" (1 Sam. 17:28-29 KJV). They could not imagine what this kid was doing there. Likewise, 1 Samuel 17:33 tells us that King Saul assumed that because of David's young age he could not successfully oppose Goliath. But as we all know, David was victorious!

Let us examine the battle in more detail. In 1 Samuel 17:38–39, we find that David did not use Saul's weapons; 1 Samuel 17:40 tells us that he used the weapons the Lord had trained him to use. And 1 Samuel 17:48 says that David was not timid in approaching Goliath, but ran toward him. Israel benefited from the action of this young warrior.

Later David was still facing giants: "Moreover the Philistines had yet war again with Israel; and David went down, and his servants with him, and fought against the Philistines: and David waxed faint. And Ishbi-benob, which was of the sons of the giant, the weight of whose spear weighed three hundred shekels of brass in weight, he being girded with a new sword, thought to have slain David. But Abishai the son of Zeruiah succored him, and smote the Philistine, and killed him. Then the men of David swear unto him, saying, Thou shall go no more out with us to battle, that thou quench not the light of Israel" (2 Sam. 21:15–17 KJV). Abishai rescues David from the giant because David had trained others to do the job he was no longer physically able to do.

Different methods as well as different people were used to conquer a city or an army. As we see in Joshua 6:20, the walls of Jericho fell only when the Israelites marched around the city, blew trumpets, and shouted. This was in direct response to God's command to Joshua. The New Testament, in Revelation 19:1 and John 12:13, also tells us to praise God with a shout. Hebrews 5:7 tells us that Jesus often prayed to God using loud cries and supplications. I believe that the Lord is showing us in these verses that the walls protecting our spiritual enemies will likewise fall, leaving them defenseless before us, if we also will shout His praises. I believe God is well pleased with our praises. Look carefully at 2 Samuel 6:16, which tells us that King David danced with all his might as he brought the ark of the covenant, the very presence of God, back to Jerusalem. As we saw earlier, David was a perfect example of a warrior/praiser.

In Chronicles, we see the great example of a praise warrior: "They rose early in the morning, and went forth into the wilderness of Tekoa: and as they went forth, Jehoshaphat stood and said, Hear me, O Judah, and ye inhabitants of Jerusalem: Believe in the Lord your God, so shall ye be established; believe His prophets, so shall ye prosper. And when he had consulted with the people, he appointed singers unto the Lord, and that should praise the beauty of holiness, as they went out before the army, and to say, Praise the Lord; for his mercy endureth forever. And when they began to sing and to praise, the Lord set ambushments against the children of Ammon, Moab, and mount Seir, which were come against Judah; and they were smitten. For the children of Ammon and Moab stood up against the inhabitants of mount Seir, utterly to slay and destroy them: and when they had made an end of the inhabitants of Seir, every one helped to destroy another" (2 Chron. 20:20-23 KJV).

I am also reminded of Gideon's army described in Judges 7:4–8. God handpicked three hundred men whose most distinguishing characteristic was not that they had proved themselves as mighty men of valor, but that they drank water from a different position than the others. When they were in place, surrounding the Midianites' camp, Gideon and his small army blew their trumpets, shouted their battle cry, broke their pitchers, and held their torches high. "When the three hundred blew the trumpets, the Lord set every man's sword against his companion throughout the whole camp; and the [enemy] army fled to Beth Acacia" (Judges 7:22). In the dark, the Midianites panicked at the tumult of shouting, trumpet blasts and breaking pitchers, and the sight of torches surrounding them. In their terror and confusion, they fought and killed each other. Gideon's men emerged unscathed. So God, with the most insignificant man in Manasseh leading an insignificant troop, wrought a great victory for Israel. And there was peace for 40 years (Judges 8:28).

As we look at another area of warfare, we see many battles. Great books have been written on spiritual warfare, but there is one level of warfare not often mentioned. It involves God's Special Forces. Our armed forces train men to be strong against the Goliaths of our day, such as those setting up nests of machine guns and other weapons intended to take the army off guard. Our intelligence agencies are always seeking ways to wipe out these strongholds, which can do great damage with surprise attacks. The David's of World War II would say, "I will take care of those machine gun nests for the ground troops." So it is with God's Green Berets; they stand ready to go into the trouble spots and do warfare for God's people.

As we consider the methods of spiritual battle, we see that God never attempts anything without a master plan. It is up to us to know the plan for the task He asks of us. Many times we forget or get careless, thinking God will understand, but God will not allow us to be careless about what He has asked us to do. Carelessness can be devastating to us and others. David, a man after God's own heart, sent for the ark of the covenant, but it was brought in the wrong manner, with a new cart, violating God's instructions for bearing the ark. This had devastating results. Later when David searched for and found the manuscripts with the instructions, he realized <u>special people </u>were required to carry the ark. When he followed the Lord's directions and used the Levites to bear the ark, things worked out for the good. There is a workable plan in the service of the Lord.

CHAPTER 3

GOD'S NEW TESTAMENT ARMY ON EARTH

If you are living the Christian life, you are in a battle. God's people need faith and courage to fight the good fight of faith. The following Scriptures will help. We find many examples of specially trained forces in the New Testament. Again, these ordinary people surrendered themselves to God, learned the ways of heavenly warfare, and perhaps grew weary of having Satan hinder God's kingdom.

The Bible tells us about the nature of the battle: "For we do not wrestle against flesh and blood, but against the rulers, against the authorities, against the cosmic powers over this present darkness, against the spiritual forces of evil in the heavenly places" (Eph. 6:12 NIV) We don't burn down buildings where falsehood is taught or tear down night clubs, but we use the sword of the Spirit (Eph. 6:17; Heb. 4:12) to conquer the hearts of men. The kingdom of Christ was not established, nor is it defended or extended, by carnal means or by a social gospel, but by men of God who have given themselves over to God and are mighty in Him.

Scripture also discusses the nature of God's army. We were not drafted or forced to serve, but we willingly chose to be soldiers, so there should be no shirking on our part when duty calls. The cause is well defined, and there is much to fight for as we stand for truth against error and sin (1 Tim. 6:12). An army is lost without adequate leadership, but in our battles we have an infallible captain. Our captain is "King of kings and Lord of lords" (Rev. 7:14; 19:11). Moreover, we are fighting as allies on the side of all those who take their stand for truth (1 Cor. 3:5–7). If we are to win the spiritual battles in this life, we must be spiritually prepared.

Finally, there is the nature of the soldier. A good soldier endures harsh conditions. No matter how hot or tough the battle may become, we must persevere (Heb. 12:2–3). No matter how busy we are with the affairs of this life, we must always be ready for duty (Titus 2:14; 3:1, 14). We must always please the commanding officer. Christ is the captain of His army, and we must obey His orders (Matt. 7:21–23).

Ephesians 6:13–14 urges us to don "the whole armor of God" and "the girdle of truth." A huge leather girdle or belt that went about the midsection (similar to what a prizefighter wears) was the foundation of a Roman soldier's armor. This foundation for the Christian soldier is the truth—without it, there is no need to fight the battle. It is the basis for all that we do. The Roman soldier was expected to fight in battle for as many as seventy-two hours without relief. The truth will enable us to stand and prevail. The "breastplate of righteousness" (Eph. 6:14) hooks into the girdle of truth to form one unified piece of armor. This is the righteousness that comes only through Jesus Christ (Phil. 3:9). Without righteousness, we will never be able to fight the battle. We cannot influence others and win souls to Christ unless we are what we claim to be. At times what we do speaks more loudly than what we say.

Ephesians 6:15 tells us our feet must be shod with the "gospel of peace." The Roman soldier did not enter battle in Italian sandals, but in heavy bronze boots. God wants our feet to be shod with the gospel, because we will be marching on rough terrain. Leading us in battle is the captain of the heavenly host as seen in Joshua 5:13–6:5. The captain of the host of the Lord God led the people of Israel across the Jordan into the Promised Land.

Being trained in the Lord calls for a strong prayer life, knowing the Scriptures, and having faith in God. It also entails going through many trying times, facing many dangers, and suffering persecution. Many are being prepared for special work in God's kingdom but are not yet aware of it. If you would like to be this kind of warrior, today is a great day to start. Prayer is required for any service for God, and yet prayer will not always be all that is required. It is important to learn the Scripture so that when you are assigned to a task you will have good knowledge of the methods God uses.

We will endure various trials while God trains us for His service. Jesus talks about learning obedience through suffering. Training is not easy, yet not all of our suffering is for training. I believe God often uses suffering for good even though it is frequently the result of our faults and failures. We have to suffer, sometimes because of circumstances such as natural disasters, and yet many times God will use even these for our good. We must develop a faith in the One whom we serve, so we will not become discouraged while in training. We are often tempted to give up when conflicts arise. Just as soldiers must go through training that simulates real battle to prepare for war, so must we.

Where there is a battle, there is an enemy. The enemy we face is the devil, known as Lucifer. He is referred to in Ezekiel 28:14-19 KJV:

Thou art the anointed cherub that covereth; and I have set thee so: thou wast upon the holy mountain of God; thou hast walked up and down in the midst of the stones of fire. Thou wast perfect in thy ways from the day that thou wast created, till iniquity was found in thee. By the multitude of thy merchandise they have filled the midst of thee with violence, and thou hast sinned: therefore I will cast thee as profane out of the mountain of God: and I will destroy thee, O covering cherub, from the midst of the stones of fire. Thine heart was lifted up because of thy beauty, thou hast corrupted thy wisdom by reason of thy brightness: I will cast thee to the ground, I will lay thee before kings, that they may behold thee. Thou hast defiled thy sanctuaries by the multitude of thine iniquities, by the iniquity of thy traffick; therefore will I bring forth a fire from the midst of thee, it shall devour thee, and I will bring thee to ashes upon the earth in the sight of all them that behold thee. All they that know thee among the people shall be astonished at thee: thou shalt be a terror, and never shalt thou be any more.

Little is said about this Lucifer in the Old Testament, but under various names we find him throughout the Scriptures, especially in the New

Testament where he is known as Beelzebub, Satan, the Prince of Darkness and by many other titles. The very first thing we need to note is that whoever or whatever this Lucifer is, he is being cast down from all places *heaven!* Some have just stopped here and declared, "What else do we need? This Lucifer was 'in' heaven!" But we must look at more than the use of just one word before establishing and believing a doctrine.

Isaiah 14:12–15 says, "How art thou fallen from heaven, O Lucifer, son of the morning! How art thou cut down to the ground, which didst weaken the nations! For thou hast said in thine heart, I will ascend into heaven, I will exalt my throne above the stars of God: I will sit also upon the mount of the congregation, in the sides of the north: I will be like the most High. Yet thou shalt be brought down to hell, to the sides of the pit."

Some would say, "How could a human expect to ascend into heaven?" This is a sign to some that this Lucifer is a spirit-being capable of entering heaven. Next, we find this being has a throne. We can surmise that the throne was given to him by a superior force or entity—the only possible choice, by God Himself. Not only does Lucifer have a throne, which means power and dominion over a realm of some sort, but he also wants to extend it "above" the stars of God Himself. Now, whatever those "stars" may be, this is surely blasphemous thinking! Would it not be fair to state that this line of thinking reveals to us that Lucifer is full of vanity? He thought he was pretty hot stuff.

Finally, Isaiah 14:14 says that Lucifer intends to rise up over the clouds. Since he was banished to earth, that would appear to be simple enough to understand, but notice that he says, "I will be like the most High." In the Hithpael Verb Stem in Hebrew, the verb specifically means *to make oneself like.* This being is so vain that he thinks he can be as God to the earth and its inhabitants! This verb does not mean that he will become God, just that he will appear to be God.

Let us move quickly to God's armies, which are greater in power than Satan's, and see the two in battle. "'Go, find out where he is, the king ordered, so I can send men and capture him.' The report came back: 'He is in Dothan.' Then he sent horses and chariots and a strong force there. They went by night and surrounded the city. When the servant of the man of God got up and went out early the next morning, an army with horses and chariots had surrounded the city. 'Oh, my lord, what shall we do?' the servant asked. 'Don't be afraid,' the prophet answered. 'Those who are with us are more than those who are with them.' And Elisha prayed, 'O Lord open his eyes so he may see.' Then the Lord opened the servant's eyes, and he looked and saw the hills full of horses and chariots of fire all around Elisha" (2 Kings 6:13-17 NIV).

Mighty armies of heaven are led by the great captain of heaven. All the powers of heaven are at your disposal through Jesus Christ, who said, "Put your sword back into its place; for all those who take up the sword shall perish by the sword. Or do you think that I cannot appeal to My Father, and He will at once put at my disposal more than twelve legions of angels?" (Matt. 26:52–53).

Joshua 5:13–14 offers an excellent example of a heavenly intervention: "And it came to pass, when Joshua was by Jericho, that he lifted his eyes and looked, and behold, a Man stood opposite him with His sword drawn in His hand. And Joshua went to Him and said to Him, 'Are you for us or for our adversaries?' So He said, 'No, but as Commander of the army of the Lord I have now come.'"

Joshua's question reveals a typical mind-set that poses a threat to our effectiveness in the service of the Savior in the church today. We tend to see the battles we face as our battles and the forces we face as forces marshaled against us and our individual causes, concerns, agendas, and even our theological beliefs or positions on doctrine. And in a sense that is so if we are truly standing in the cause of Christ.

All those serving that cause have their places in the hierarchy of heaven, with God being the head. Christ is our redeemer, the Holy Spirit our guide. Angels have their ranks and duties. The seraphim work in the spiritual realm, while the cherubim are guardians of the throne and often carry out judgment. Other types we call common angels, but they are not at all common, since they minister to the saints and at the end time will bind Satan. They seem to have had a large part in the creation. Job 38 records several groups of them worshiping and singing at the completion of creation, and all through the Bible, they are involved in the affairs of man. In Revelation, they play a major part in the end-time judgment and in reaping the harvest. Seraphim have six wings. Next are the cherubim, who have four wings. They also cover God's throne. They guard over God's children and are very active in His kingdom.

Another description of God's armies is found in Hebrews 1:7, where we learn that He "maketh his angels' spirits and His ministers a flame of fire." In this, we see a reason for the commander's description of himself as the captain of the Lord's host: he was assuring Joshua of his provision through a mighty angelic army.

A final example of God's angelic armies and their ministry to His people is seen in Hebrews 1:14, which reads: "Are they not all ministering spirits, sent out to render service for the sake of those who will inherit the kingdom?" Throughout the book of Revelation, we find God's angelic armies carrying out His judgments and mercies.

We often wonder why there is so much confusion in the world today. Is it just that men are mean or could it be that the forces of hell are ruling this world through people who surrender to Satan? In Ephesians, we find how Satan is working today to destroy us. Just like God, he must have people who will allow him to work through them. Ephesians 6:12 gives us a list of Satan's organized angelic armies: "For we wrestle not against flesh and blood, but against principalities, against powers, against the rulers of the darkness of this world, against spiritual wickedness in high places."

These are the evil armies of the unseen world, and great is their power. Perhaps these principalities and powers remain mostly in the citadel of the kingdom of darkness, but other evil spirits range abroad, committed to the provinces of the world. These spirits continually oppose faith, love, and holiness, either by force or fraud, and labor to infuse unbelief, pride, idolatry, malice, envy, anger, and hatred.

Satan set his claim on this world at the fall of man and has become progressively more wicked in his attacks through the ages. Now at what is seemingly the end of this age, more evil is being set before the eyes of everyone, particularly the young. More tools of evil are appearing in this new age of technology to capture hearts and minds. Jesus said in Matthew 24:22, "And except those days should be shortened, there should no flesh be saved." Regiments of evil spirits are roaming the world today, looking for those they can deceive, confuse, and disorient spiritually. They are in opposition to the church, and with well-organized armies, they attack anywhere God is being exalted (and many other places). A few of these spirits are called by name, character, or duties. There are group titles according to their abilities. May God enlighten your mind to see the devastation that is planned against His kingdom, the government, church, and the home.

When the Word speaks of a certain group of these powers, it is most likely an army of vast numbers. We do not have a number concerning the good angels. Hebrews 12:22 ESV. says, "But you have come to Mount Zion and to the city of the living God, the heavenly Jerusalem, and to innumerable angels in festal gathering." Angels that are part of heaven's armies are probably what God uses to fight our battles after we have committed things into His hands. The book of Revelation speaks of angels round the throne ten thousand times ten thousands. Jesus says He could have called ten thousand angels to destroy the earth and set men free.

The book of Job speaks of angels called sons of God rejoicing at the creation of the earth: "Where wast thou when I laid the foundations of the earth? declare, if thou hast understanding. Who hath laid the measures thereof, if thou knowest? or who hath stretched the line upon it? Whereupon are the foundations thereof fastened? or who laid the corner stone thereof; When the morning stars sang together, and all the sons of God shouted for joy?" (Job 38:5–7) Daniel records how the angels fought their way through an evil angel, the prince of Persia, to bring the answer to Daniel's prayer. This makes me believe that principalities confront the people in other places. So as we consider the multiple trillions of these beings, we must realize that the powers of hell cannot be controlled by natural means, only by the power that Jesus left with us. When He went away, He made sure we were aware of the means whereby we could conquer the enemy.

Let us look more closely at each of the four deadly armies, their nature, and duties.

First, there are principalities, which seem to be chief rulers of the unseen world system, first in rank or first in existence, doling out unholy orders to other evil spirits. The antichrist spirit, the spoiler, the plunderer, harasses you to the point where you want to give up. This spirit is a troublemaker in the church, the world, and the home. Spiritual warfare for the Christian is about the struggle between truth and falsehood, love and hate, and good and evil, and relying on the integrity of God's Word. These elements are experienced in the realms of the world, in the flesh, the devil, and his evil spirits.

God did not leave us helpless. In Christ, we are more than conquerors. Our weapons of warfare are found in the wisdom of Christ: God's Word and Holy Spirit despoiling the principalities and the powers. Christ "made a public spectacle of them, leading them away in triumph by it" (Col. 2:15), for in Him were created all things in heaven and on earth, the visible and the invisible, whether thrones or dominions or principalities or powers; all things were created through Him and for Him. "Put on the whole armor of God that ye may be able to stand against the wiles of the devil," says Ephesians 6:11. "The heavens are Thine, the earth also is Thine, as for the world and the fullness thereof, Thou hast founded them. The north and the south Thou hast created them" (Ps. 89:11–12 KJV). There is a wonderful passage in Paul's epistles that we should write in letters of gold on our chamber walls: "No temptation has overtaken you except what is common to humanity. God is faithful and He will not allow you to be tempted beyond what you are able, but with the temptation He will also provide a way of escape, so that you are able to endure it." (1 Corinthians 10:13)

Second are the powers. The enemy's intention is to rob us of our power and energy. They are a force that extracts, removes, breaks up, and plucks out (as an eye). They want us to be lazy and inactive (a major tool). The Antichrist and the rulers of darkness use these powers to knock us off balance, by various means diverting our attention from prayer and keeping God's word. They cause us to be unbalanced in our beliefs, faithfulness to God and home, and make us unstable. They strike at the heart, try to shut the preacher's mouth, destroy the body, and get us to serve Satan with our bodies. They make the minds of men unstable and convince them to oppose God. They cause us to be spiritually unbalanced in doctrines and morals.

But consider God's power of preservation. No creature has power to preserve itself. "Can the bush grow up without mire? Can the flag grow up without water?" (Job 8:11). God is called the preserver of "man and beast" (Ps. 36:6). "He upholdeth all things by the word of His power"

(Heb. 1:3). Romans 9:22 speaks of how "God, willing to show wrath, and to make His power known, endured with much long-suffering the vessels of wrath fitted to destruction." "The Lord is the strength of my life; of whom shall I be afraid?" (Ps. 27:1). "Now unto Him that is able to do exceeding abundantly above all that we ask or think, according to the power that worketh in us, unto Him be glory in the church by Christ Jesus throughout all ages, world without end. Amen" (Eph. 3:20–21).

Third are the rulers of darkness, of the <u>world system.</u> Paul says that "the god of this world hath blinded the minds of them which believe not, lest the light of the glorious gospel of Christ, who is the image of God, should shine unto them, not the earth" (2 Cor. 4:4). The earth is the Lord's and the fullness therein. Hades is the abode of the dead. Witchcraft darkens minds, especially those of the young. Likewise, black magic, obscurity, and obscenity bring unhappiness.

Paul declares: "For I am persuaded that neither death nor life, nor angels nor principalities nor powers, nor things present nor things to come" can separate us from God's love (Rom. 8:38 KJV). Matthew 6:23 asks, "If there be darkness how great is that darkness?" The Antichrist is active, but "Now is the judgment of this world; now the ruler of this world will be cast out" (John 12:31). Daniel 7:25 says, "He shall speak pompous words against the Most High, shall persecute the saints of the Most High, and shall intend to change times and law. Then the saints shall be given into his hand for a time and times and half a time." We are told in 1 John 4:1 "Beloved, do not believe every spirit, but test the spirits, whether they are of God; because many false prophets have gone out into the world."

Last we have spiritual wickedness. The Greek word for wickedness is *ponēria* and means depravity, particularly in the sense of malice and mischief, plots, sins, and iniquity (*Strong's Greek Dictionary*).

Iniquity often is a gross injustice done to someone. This spirit is devastating and powerful in our day. Its primary purpose is to destroy the church, the family, the government, and the world. Using many malicious methods such as, idol worship and psychic pursuits, this spirit plots against God and man. It corrupts, perverts God's Word, and debases with lewdness and pornography; it is licentious, sexually unrestrained, immoral, and deceitful. Where it abounds, the love of many will wax cold. It promotes a Jezebel spirit in women, encouraging them to control men and weak people, especially those in leadership. It makes people do things they ought not to do and things they wish they had not done. This destroyer seeks to undermine government, desiring to have control; it foments wars and fighting, causes church splits, confusion, and shallowness. It delights in pew warmers, divided homes, and frayed family relationships. It kills babies, mutilates bodies, and makes others look bad to make itself look good. Through education, it seeks to train the young to be anti-God and anti-government.

Raging powers are causing families to dissolve. When this rage first started, the church would say, "As goes the home so goes the church and country." But that is not what I am hearing today. Pastors must not trade the truth for a large audience.

This battle takes place in the heart and soul. Satan uses temptation, oppression, obsession, and possession. He works in the realm of the mind. Victory verses can be found in Luke 4:36, Psalm 91: 10–11, Matthew 9:32–33, 12:29, 16:19 and 2 Corinthians 10:3–4. When we see these spirits working in our home, church, and world, we have authority to control them. Jesus said all power was given to Him in heaven and in earth, and then He said, "Behold! I give unto you power to tread on serpents."

Believers must not ignore spiritual wickedness in high places. Pastors must preach the whole counsel of God in the face of deception. False teachings of the occult and doctrines of demons must be identified. Believers are not to participate in the "unfruitful works of darkness" but rather should expose them. We are told that Solomon loved the Lord, walking in the statutes of David his father, but that he sacrificed and burnt incense in high places to strange gods. And Deuteronomy 12:2 warns: "Ye shall utterly destroy all the places, wherein the nations which ye shall possess served their gods, upon the high mountains, and upon the hills, and under every green tree."

Paul was aware of the evil of his day and the need for the gospel: "Unto me, who am less than the least of all saints, is this grace given, that I should preach among the Gentiles the unsearchable riches of Christ; and to make all men see what is the fellowship of the mystery, which from the beginning of the world hath been hid in God, who created all things by Jesus Christ: to the intent that now unto the principalities and powers in heavenly places might be known by the church the manifold wisdom of God" (Eph 3:8–10 KJV).

On rare occasions, we find men and women who are not afraid of these opposing forces. I would like to share an example of these powers in action. A certain woman, who chooses not to give her name, has written about how she feels God is teaching her to be a warrior in His army. I believe her story will give some of you a better insight into the spirit realm. I witnessed this story. The situations are not prevalent in every home or church, and yet it is possible for this to occur from time to time. When you hear about several people with this problem, it may sound as if it is an everyday occurrence; however, just like everyone does not have a dreadful disease, neither does everyone have her problem. I want to share these stories with the ones God is training to be in this type of ministry because people under these attacks desperately need deliverance. This is her story.

That morning was the same as other mornings. I was preparing coffee for the two of us just before leaving for work. Unaware of what was happening, I was astonished by an outburst of unusual swearing and rage in the bedroom. My mind flashed back to that first visit to his father's house several years before and hearing the identical swearing and rage. At that point the phone rang, which was unusual at that time of the morning. The voice on the other end of the line said, "Your husband's dad has just died." God instantly said to me, "The evil spirits that have controlled his dad so many years have come to harass your husband. The spirits were seeking somewhere to go, and he was the most vulnerable."

As I prayed, things got a little better but were not altogether the same as before. I am not saying they were demon-possessed; the devil can take control of the emotional part of a person if he does not know how to guard against it.

Several years passed without another outburst, when at about the same time of the morning that my husband's dad had died, I heard the anger and swearing again. I did not understand. As years before, I was pondering what was happening when the phone rang. It was my sister-in-law telling me that her husband, my husband's brother, had just died.

Again I knew in my spirit it was the same thing that happened when his dad died.

These spirits try to latch on to a person's emotions and take control, perhaps not of their spirits but of their actions. I call it a family curse. This happened again many years later when my son-in-law, who seemed to be a committed Christian, died. From time to time, he displayed fierce anger with people whom he could not control, and he would threaten to commit suicide when the family would not do what he thought it should. (I believe he brought his untimely death on himself by the words of his mouth; Proverbs says, "Life and death is in the power of the tongue.")

The day he passed away, most of his family was sitting in the living room, and my granddaughter, who was fifteen years old, began to rage just like I had heard her dad do many times. Not cursing—just displaying anger for everything and everybody. And I knew that it was those spirits that had come from his uncontrolled nature that Satan was exploiting to attack her soul.

At that time I still did not know how to deal with that type of outburst. It takes more than prayer. It takes enforcing authority over the spirits to drive them out. Since then, I have studied and have dealt with and conquered those demonic powers in many people. I have been praying for my granddaughter and have grieved for her. . I have been waiting for the right time to set her free because I am quite sure that without claiming God's deliverance she cannot help some of what she is doing. I don't think it is her true nature.

These spirits stir their victims up from time to time; the time when they are calm most likely reflects the person's true nature. These spirits are trying to take God's people out of His kingdom. That very thing has happened with my granddaughter, who was a dedicated Christian. But in the months that followed, Satan took advantage of her, and she turned away from God to do things that were not right. When a person acts like that, it surely is not from God. When a person is out of control, it is not the person's nature. It is a spirit-controlled nature.

The final story I want to tell concerns how I came to understand the power of Satan when he is unrestrained and at liberty to do what he desires to us. I became determined to learn all I could about how to help people in the same situations. With those experiences and with friends already ministering in that area, and with the help of God, I will do my best for Him and the victims. At the death of my husband, I began to notice that my taste had changed and I experienced a loss of appetite like he had when he was very ill. Someone told me that I was just sympathetic and that sometimes happened. I lost 30 pounds in a short time and my attitude was like his had been.

My brother came to visit me from another city during that time, and a friend of mine was there. My brother stopped me in the middle of a conversation and said, "This is not you talking." My friend chimed in and said, "I wanted to say that but was afraid to." They prayed for me, but it did not free me.

It takes more than prayer to bring deliverance. We must deal directly with the spirit. So I asked God to show me what to do, because for every problem there is a solution. He told me to get five smooth stones because I was now facing a giant. This would be the first time I had dealt directly with a demon. He told me to summon five righteous people and use a large bottle of oil to anoint myself and the entire house and to denounce any demonic activity in the house or in me. God told me the names of the five persons, and I called them, set up a time, and explained all that was happening. When we had done the anointing and denounced Satan's activities, all was back to normal. The problem is not that the devil is not subject to us; it is that we do not know how to take our authority. This is something that not everyone understands, so we need to know whom to call for help in time of need.

My husband had become a Christian who loved and highly respected the Lord for several years before his death. Yet he never completely got free from some of the devil's tricks.

I hope you will be better informed after reading about these experiences and will be able to dislodge evil spirits from those affected. Fasting and prayer are needed to control such attacks. When a person is suffering from an attack, it is the normal thing to judge him as being unreasonable or obeying the devil. But it could be more than that. It might be a misunderstood situation, so we should try to stay away from some people rather than deliver them. And to deliver them we must be sensitive to the Holy Spirit to know whether we are dealing with a man failing to control his sinful nature or a man under the attack of the enemy. In these last days, these situations will become more and more prevalent, and God is trying to raise up people willing to take control in these cases.

Here is a prophecy I would like to share with you from Bill Burns' *THE TRUMPET* of April 26, 2010,, from the *Spirit of Prophecy Bulletin:*

Rise up, my children, for indeed it is written and it has been spoken and it is true that the battle belongs to the Lord, because it is my battle; I will go with you, and I will strengthen you and teach you how to make war. I shall bring my battle plans into your mind and I will reveal the plans of the enemy to you. You shall be able to go forth with a heart that is set on victory and a mind that knows the reality that if I am for you it does not matter who is against you. For indeed you are my battle-axes, but the battle belongs to the Lord. So, I will lead and guide you. You are not in this alone. Take courage and take heart and rise up for you are crossing through the wilderness into the promises.

Rise up and receive the fullness of your inheritance for I am with you. I have made a way for you and established the boundaries of your habitation. I am in charge of your times of visitations and I will send you into war at the appropriate time and equip you for that victory. Yours is to simply follow with a willing and obedient heart and to receive all that I have to teach you. These are the days of the manifestation of the glory of God's Kingdom and the army that has been spoken of by the prophet Joel will now begin to arise into fullness and the victory shall be theirs. So come and go as I send you. Be one with me. Follow me absolutely for I shall walk with you on this path into the fullness of your destiny, says the Lord God Almighty.

In Matthew 28:16–20, Jesus gave us the great commission to go into the world, preaching and teaching the Word and making disciples of all. In Genesis, the Word tells us that the earth has been given to mankind and that as believers we are to subdue it for the glory of God. In Joshua 1:2, God told the Israelites to go in and possess the land He had given to Abraham, Isaac, and Jacob. To possess the Promised Land, the Israelites first had to dispossess, or drive out, and destroy the Canaanites who had usurped their territory. Matthew 12:29 tells us to bind the strong man before laying claim to his possessions. And a literal reading of Matthew

16:19 tells us to bind on earth that which has been bound in heaven. As such, we are to confront the spirits of darkness that have plagued man in the past and continue to do so today. Just as God's warriors tore down the altars of Baal set up by the Israelites who had turned to idolatry, the church today needs spiritual Green Berets to fight battles with Satan and help carry out God's plan.

Chapter 4

Digging in with God

Foxholes hold many terrible memories for soldiers who fought in the wars of the past. I cringe to think of the fears some might have faced in those hours, and I salute them for their bravery and for the price they had to pay for our freedom. Yes, the price paid for our freedom from the devil was more dreadful than what our men suffered, but freedom always has a cost.

The price I had to pay to be used by God in ministry was many years of suffering rejection, facing torrents of demons, and learning how to be victorious over the enemy, never retreating from a seemingly impossible battle. Any thought of giving in had to be banished. Forty-eight years of training brought strength and the ability to know my God and his faithfulness better, along with knowing my enemy so I would know which one was attacking me. It is important to follow the pattern of the Bible to combat these forces. Before you can manifest power over the devil, you must be born again. Then you have to prepare, but just because we are not prepared and fail does not mean it cannot be done. And just because we don't understand a situation, or have not been taught how we can be free, does not make the task impossible. I believe this book will help you see into God's Word and understand His plan. I would like to share parts of my life to show you how to develop a strong prayer life and an intimate relationship with God.

RUTH LEE

As I was moved from one duty to another and saw others who were stable in their ministry, I asked God what part I had in His kingdom. He said the words "Green Beret." But I knew very little about them. I had met a man once who was part of the Special Forces, but he did not tell me anything about what he did. Therefore, I began a study and found it quite interesting how the Green Berets are trained for their mission. As I share a small part of my Christian life, I will show you how I was prepared to do some of the things I do now, unaware of what God was doing in my life at the time. Learning about the different types of warfare will help us understand some of the battles we face in the supernatural realm. This might explain why most of my assignments from God are very private. Only those to whom I am ministering know the situation. I want to share how God identified me as being a special force. He used one of my life experiences to help me understand.

Years ago, I was ministering to a woman who had an alcoholic husband and whose marriage was on the brink of disaster. She called one day and told me her husband had just returned home after having been gone several days. She explained what he had done that week, and she said she had all she was going to take. He had traded his good car for an older one and sold his best jacket. She said she was on her way to retrieve the automobile and asked if I would go with her. I did and discovered that a man who ran a bar and pool hall had the car.

An angry woman is more dangerous than the devil realizes. Without hesitation, we marched into that place, and she did not ask for the car but said she had come to get it. An awestruck man quickly got the keys and gave them to her. She gave him the keys to the old car.

After we returned home, I began to sense God's presence, and spontaneously I began to acknowledge God's power throughout the heavens and earth. I was turning around and round. Then I stopped and began to call the demonic powers that had been influencing the woman's husband into my living room. Not a fear or doubt was present. They lined up across the side of the room. There seemed to be about nine or ten. I could see them, but I do not think it was with my eyes. I believe I was seeing them with my spirit, but they were there. I began to tell them what part of the world to go to, and gave them a command never to return, them or any others like them. They never uttered a word because I had had enough of them, having heard all they had done to that family. They knew it. Then I sent them away.

God told me He had prepared the man to receive Jesus and for me to go lead him into the kingdom. I called the wife and told her I was coming, but she was hesitant because he had such a hangover. Well do you think that would stop me? I rushed over, and they were sitting at the dining table. I wasted no time. I told the man, "God has sent me to lead you to Jesus," and he said, "I know." And he received Christ that moment. Through the years, I have asked him if he had ever desired another drink and he has always said, "Never!" He was totally delivered that day and is in church, living for Jesus. This is what I mean when I say my work is a secretive thing: I will never tell who the person is and most likely will never tell the story again.

All of my young life I was taught and trained in the ways of the Lord and knew Him. Then, at the age of sixteen, I departed from Him for fifteen years. Through the prayers of my family and friends, the Holy Spirit began to nudge my heart and strongly convicted me of my sins. That is when I gave my life to God; never to be the same again as I delved into the work I had been taught and began to study the kingdom of God and the kingdom of Satan. Not knowing at that time what God's plans were for me, I still followed His directions, which has paid great dividends.

I still needed spiritual help upon my return, and within weeks God sent me a mentor to guide me in my attempt to find the Lord. I was instructed to take my Bible, a Bible dictionary, and a commentary and begin to read. To my amazement, the Word was already alive to me. I credit that to my godly parents, who taught me the Word in my formative years. Time passed, and after attending all the prayer meetings I could find and listening intently to the preaching of the Word. God took me another step.

Looking back now to when God first used me, I realize that He has been faithful, speaking to me and through me for many years. When I was a child, our family lived on a small farm. I was enjoying some private time with my mother one evening when I was about eleven years old. As night approached, my dad had ridden into town in a wagon to buy a horse. My mother was a very caring person, and she was concerned when my dad did not come home. It was getting dark. She realized he could not see very well, and she became more bothered as time passed, so I suppose God wanted to console her a little.

I believe He used me to do that. God was speaking to me. This was my first vision. I told my mom not to worry, that I knew exactly where my dad was. For about an hour, I mentioned every turn he made and every house, he passed describing his position. When he got in sight of the house, I told her to go to the window and look because he was coming around the next corner. She looked and was astonished to find him right where I told her he was. It just seemed normal to me, but she wanted to know how I knew all of that.

God spoke again when I was twenty-one years old, this time about my relationship with Him and about my lifestyle. I had departed from my faith in God and was living a life not pleasing to Him. I ran from God and even turned on the church, and then the night visions began. This is the way God got my attention. The night was a night of horror, but because I always had a high respect for God, it started me in a different direction. God came to me that night, and there were billows of flame surrounding me as far as I could see, in every direction and overhead. Only a narrow path was open, and the Lord spoke to me in no uncertain terms. He said, "You can leave through the opening or be eternally lost. This is the only time you have, and the only path out for you."

I was startled. I went into the kitchen, sat down, and pondered what I had just experienced. I made a decision to turn from that way of life the best way I knew how. I did everything within my ability, but at the time I did not know about God's ability. Self-righteousness is not what God desires for us. However, He knew my future and was helping me find my way. I did not repent at that point, but that night started me on a right course.

God spoke to me several times through the years. Then, several years later when I was trying to return to the Lord, He began speaking to me again in dreams. At this point, God began to speak to me in my spirit—we had a long conversation that first day. And He did so until the day I gave my heart to Him. He challenged me with a strong question: "What would you give to be saved?" I was so tired of sin and so fearful of being lost forever that I said, "I will give everything I have—my family, my home, whatever it takes." That day I said, "If you will help me, I will do what you say. If you do not help, I cannot do it." That day I was born again by the Spirit of God.

So, for God to speak to me is not unusual as long as I am living according to his Word and doing all the things I should. That is what keeps the line to heaven open. I talk to God and He speaks to me on regular basis. He said, "Call and I will answer." Why don't you try it if you are not already talking to Him? I cannot comprehend the grace of God, how He is so long-suffering, waiting on a person for so many years to come to Him, but I am thankful.

From my youth, I was taught the Word through various means—my parents, my church, and a few books. It was important for me to commit some of the Word to memory. I was taught early in my life to make sure to learn directly from the Word rather than just from what men said about it. Though there are many good pastors, teachers, and books that can be a great help and an inspiration, we must allow the final teaching to be from God's Word. My dad was my example of a true Christian. Being a minister, he was an ardent student of the Bible. I'm told that he read the Bible through almost 50 times, committing it to memory, to the point where he could quote it verbatim. Having that kind of example when I became a believer was a great help.

I began a life of searching for God by studying every day, most of the time for hours. I would rush to get my housework and duties finished so I could be alone with God and learn all I could about Him and His purpose. I continue to do this today. My main interest has been how I can please God and live according to His Word.

Having studied and taught for most of my Christian life, I have taught through the Bible and am in the process of teaching through it again in Bible studies, seminars, worker training courses, and short revivals. I am always aware that I must teach the truth and not what I think is right, and I am sure I have missed the truth at times. That is why I study the whole context of the Scriptures, seeking to know what biblical figures were talking about at the time, what the culture was, and other aspects of God's Word. And there is so much I have not learned, so much I desire to know. Even the knowledge I have is not worth a lot unless the Holy Spirit makes it alive in me. In addition, through the years I have heard teachers and preachers who had not studied deep into the

Scriptures even though they had great knowledge of the Word. There was something missing in their theology.

Suffering is a part of Christian life. Early in my walk with God, at times I would become weary wondering if the trials would ever end. The Word came alive to me and brought peace. After you have suffered awhile, the Spirit said, God would establish, strengthen, and settle you. He promised He would always be there and would never forsake us. He will find a way to help us through a Scripture, a friend, or a minister; we must always be ready to receive His help.

If you are reading this book, you most likely desire spiritual insight. Perhaps unaware of a deeper experience, you can have with God, when in prayer; ask Him if there is something beyond where you are with Him. There is always more, no matter how great our relationship is with the Lord or what our service is to Him. Ask Him to reveal to you; ask Him to lead you to it. How can you go wrong with that?

God used a minister on television to inspire me to intensify my prayer life. He was challenging people to pray a specific prayer an hour a day. That was difficult for me at the time because my family was home and my husband had retired. Still I devoted myself to an hour of special prayer beyond my regular prayer times. I would retreat to a picnic table, which was very public, and sit for one hour, just developing an intimate relationship with God. It was amazing how no one ever came to sit with me, which was unusual. My husband almost always joined me wherever I was. Amazingly enough, he never came while I was in prayer. It makes me wonder if he knew what I was doing, even though I was just sitting quietly, with no evidence that I was praying. But you know how husbands are—they just seem to know.

These times had an awesome impact on my life; I became even more intent in prayer and learning. This led to many answers to prayer, some miracles, and many trials. One of the miracles was particularly astounding...

MY MOTHER'S HEALING

Aware that my mother had an untreatable brain tumor, I began to intercede for her. I had seen miracles happen before but not of this magnitude. Doctors had sent her home to die, and she was informed that within three weeks she would begin to see webs before her eyes. She was told she would die within about two months, but as I prayed that night, God began to speak to me about a miracle for my mother.

I inquired of the Lord how He would like me to carry out His plan. His instructions were to tell my mother how to begin eating again. It had been quite a while since she could eat anything but crackers. At that time, we had only one car, and my husband used it for his job all day every day. That presented a problem, but God began to speak to my heart and let me know that all I needed to do was ask. I asked my husband if it was possible for me to have the car for a day, and he said that I could. God had already gone before me and made a way. Oh! What a God!

On my way to her house that day, I cleansed my heart and mind of anything that I was thinking and any plan that might hinder God's, and by the time I arrived, my heart was ready. With my mother being sick for so many years with a tumor on her pituitary gland, it would be interesting to see how God convinced her to receive His plan; however, as always, He had prepared her.

I was not polished in my delivery of God's messages, so I walked in and asked her to sit down. I told her that I had a message from God and told her that He had sent her a miracle. I told her that He was healing her brain tumor and that she was to start eating very slowly. I had no doubt about her receiving the miracle. I just knew it and felt confident that God was in control. She received the miracle gladly, and none of the things happened that the doctors had said would happen.

Years later when my mother had some headaches, a doctor told her that the tumor was becoming active again, and a spiritual anger arose in me. I defied those words in the name of the living God. A neurologist in my hometown examined her for two or three days and sent the tests off. A few days later, he called me into the room and began to explain that an impossible thing had happened. The tumor had shrunk to the size of a dried lady pea and could not cause her any problems. It was a mystery to him because she could not take the necessary treatments. James says, "The prayer of faith shall save the sick and the Lord will raise him up."

She lived on for several years, and the brain tumor never bothered her again.

One day when she was cooking breakfast, she fell and broke her hip and went into shock from which she died. I sat in the hospital with her the last three days of her life although she could not communicate. On the third night she became very restless, groaning for every breath. She began to calm down as I walked over to her bed and sang "Amazing Grace." After a while, I stopped and she became very uncomfortable again. I started singing again and she relaxed. This went on all night; it was about five in the morning when I realized her breathing was slowing down. I called the nurse and the family, but she was gone in a few minutes. I was relieved because it was not good for her to suffer as much as she had. God was with us in the process of her burial, and I know it was God's grace that carried us through.

PARTNERS IN PRAYER

God calls us from time to time to move to another level in the Spirit. Sharon and I were prayer partners, and it seemed we desired the same thing in prayer. We set a special time to get together to seek God. When we joined together to pray it developed into the most awesome time of my life. God began to bring change, and restoration to people's lives when we joined together against the enemy of the soul. We prayed sincerely, and within a short time, others heard and began to join us.

I was one of the first to realize I had moved away from the type of ministry in which God had used me for so many years. My ministry earlier in my Christian walk was to reveal weaknesses in others and help them overcome these faults. I showed them how to combat demonic powers that had invaded their homes and lives and to develop stick-to-itiveness in their marriages. As I began to confess my own slackness in service to God, He began to restore my spiritual boldness. I saw that truth is far better than a pat on the back. I thought I had been too direct with people. Others were always encouraging people, while I was confronting them with their faults. But He showed me how many more people I had helped by doing what I did rather than being superficial and offering the words they wanted to hear. I was called to die to myself, take up my cross, and follow Him. I had run from that calling for several years, but that was not right. Remember Jonah?

It became a saying. "If they come to Ruth for help, they are surely ready to change." It is a normal thing for people to shy away from a confrontation, especially if there is sin in their lives or if they have deviated from the Word. I still hesitate at times, knowing what I say will not be accepted, but the grace of God helps me to do what I know He is telling me to do.

As we would gather each week determined to find a private getaway from the toils of this life, we could hardly wait for our 8:30 starting time. Sometimes Sharon would be early. No time was wasted. We would put on some music, worship, and seek God's heart. Once again I started searching my mind to see if my thinking aligned with God's Word, and to my surprise, He began to reveal things that were a hindrance to me and others. I began to give my thoughts to the Lord day after day, and even if it takes awhile to continue purging my thoughts, what God has helped me do already is wonderful! I am experiencing the peace that right thinking can give. It helps us to understand people and their faults better so we will not be as judgmental, and it helps us to be able to love the unlovely.

Astounding things happen when you begin surrendering to God. You begin to move into the impossible realm. This is the supernatural. You will be asked to do things that are utterly impossible, or so you think.

It was a time like this when I had a desire to teach, but did not know where. I prayed and told God I would do whatever he wanted me to do. Suddenly a vision began, in the middle of the day. I saw a television studio. Since I had never been inside one, I knew what it was only because I could see what was taking place there. I was hosting a Bible teaching show, and two friends whom I held in high esteem were my guests. One was a male prophecy teacher, and the other was a female Sunday school teacher.

I rushed to the house of the lady who was to be my co-host and told her what I had just experienced. We both thought it was really far out. So no more was said about it until a year later, when I had the same vision and was told it was no laughing matter. Not knowing what to do, I waited to see if anything else occurred. Then one morning at work, I was talking to a gentleman, unaware of his occupation as a youth pastor. We were discussing teaching. I said that I would really like to teach but no doors had opened for me. To my shock, he asked, "Ruth, why don't you teach on television?"

I was stunned; he knew nothing about my vision. I said I knew nothing about television, and he replied, "I do. I work at a television station. And I will make you an appointment with the program manager." I kept the appointment and I told her what kind of show I wanted to do, using the vision as my guide. She said, "Ruth, I wish everyone knew as much about production as you do. When can you start?" That was enough to put me in shock.

That was the beginning of a three-and-a-half-year program on that station that I produced and hosted. Earlier that year this same man approached me in church one Sunday, handed me a small piece of paper, and said, "God gave me this while I was in prayer last night." It was a short prophecy that said something like this: God has a plan to take you to places you will not understand to use you for His service.

After that, I moved to a Christian station and stayed there three-and-a-half years until the station was sold. There I took part in a variety show. I knew I had to get the attention of non-Christians. The first part of the program would be a talk show featuring guests like doctors, lawyers, horticulturists, a governor's wife, and many more distinguished people, discussing almost every walk of life. The last part of the show involved a Bible study or a guest giving a testimony. There were shows on marriage, home, and children. If God could do that with a person like me, you can truly say that nothing is impossible with God.

I received a written paper on "soaking" that discussed how a prayer group would meet and just sit or lie before the Lord for long periods, absorbing His goodness and allowing Him to talk to them. That was what we were doing—just soaking in His presence for about an hour each time and getting closer to Him. We usually ended up with strong praise for God, and He began to bring deliverances to each one as needed. God inhabits the praises of His people. One lady who had struggled for many years one morning gave it all to Jesus, and many years later she is still free.

Some in the group began to prophesy and have visions, words of knowledge, and messages in tongues and the interpretation. Again, we grew until my family room would no longer hold the people, and we moved to the church where we would "soak" with good worship music for an hour and then come together for whatever devotion God gave us for that day. Then we would put on our praise music, and for the next hour or so, we praised with banners, flags, and small musical instruments.

Use what you have. If you want to know God's plan for your life, the best place to start is bowing before God. I realized that God's will is mainly what He reveals to you as you walk with Him day by day. Abraham left his country not knowing where he was going, but others were given specific plans, so I strongly desired to find out what He was planning for me. Even though I was already functioning in many areas of strong ministry, not always understanding how people were helped in their battles, there remained a strong desire to know more about what God expected of me.

Music was a huge part of our Wednesday morning prayer and worship in the home and at the church, and with all the instruments that we had bought, each person had something in hand to praise with as we played praise music and danced like Miriam did. We also had special gatherings that featured the shofar. The Lord seemed pleased with our worship as we learned the different sounds and how they were used in Israel.

The Hebrew word *shofar* means "a sense of incising; cutting or burning into," and it comes from a root word meaning *beauty*. The sound was more than the sound of a mere horn blast for the ancient Hebrews, who gave it a name that signified a cutting or burning into the heart and soul of the people. However, the name evoked beauty rather than harshness. Even now, most would agree that when you hear the anointed sound of the shofar, it deeply penetrates soul and spirit in a quite beautiful fashion. The shofar is normally used to seize people's attention, awakening the soul and spirit, announcing that something important is to follow. It informed the people from tribe to tribe of what was about to happen. It was as effective as Sharon's messages on the computer to the people of our church. It sounded to rally troops to battle and to announce feast days.

A sound called *teki'ah gedoiah* is one long blast. It is used to call upon God. It sounded at Mount Sinai before God's descent. This reminds us of the time when we will be called home. "For the Lord Himself will descend from heaven with a shout, with the voice of an archangel, and with the trumpet of God" (1 Thess. 4:16).

We all should be listening for this sound. Thank God for these beautiful sounds.

ANOTHER CALL TO FAST

Several years after the death of my husband Hubert, I put my house on the market, but it did not sell right away, so I used it for prayer groups and other activities. One day I went over to check on the place and be alone with God and talk to Him, and I decided I would take a small mattress and some water and go for three days of fasting and prayer. I would forgo my meal times, read the Bible, and pray instead of eating. Of course I would pray all three days, but this was to be my special time with God. God says that His word is meat and the Spirit is water. There was no food in the house, and I did not take any with me. I set a time and date.

This may sound a little far out to some of you, but this is a part of my relationship with God. I made an appointment with God to begin a three-day fast and prayer. This was a private thing even though I had many friends and prayer companions, and I kept those plans between me and God. So as I would visit the house, I would talk to Him about my plans, telling Him that I would be there on that certain day at 8:30 to spend three days with Him. I was looking forward to being with Him. I did this time after time until the day arrived. I was so excited that morning. I was going to find out what God wanted from me and not ask for anything.

I arrived that morning at 8:30 with my anointing oil to anoint the house and dedicate it to His service as I had done through the years. I went from room to room anointing every area of the house, giving it to God for His pleasure for the next few days. The presence of God was so strong in that place. That was a life-changing day in my Christian life. I told one person about what I planned to do, because she was a prayer partner, but to my amazement, before that day was over, nine people came to pray. God set His approval on that time. It would take too long to tell about the next few days. I will just say it was awesome and that much was accomplished in lives.

It was just the beginning of many other prayer meetings where people were blessed, filled with the Holy Spirit, healed, and strengthened as we moved on to larger finalities. Soon after those three days of prayer and fasting, some women in another city heard what was happening, came to see, and asked us to visit their church, which we did. Much was accomplished. Linda and I were co-teachers at that time, and we did a two-day, two-night seminar. I was speaking on the Song of Solomon as a symbol of Christ love for the church when I noticed that the back row was full of men. That was all right with me. Linda said the Lord directed her how to do the altar call because God had given her the inspiration to call for those who wanted to be filled with the Holy Spirit. That night I was told eighteen people were filled with the Holy Spirit. This was for ladies only, but the men of that church were so ready for God in their lives in a new way that they came uninvited and sat in the back row or with their wives. Most were filled with the Holy Spirit that night.

Later, we met in a large room at our church. We would begin at 9:00 a.m. and have one hour of soul-searching and getting in touch with God with soft worship music and many hungry hearts. We would then have a short devotion, and changing the music from worship to praise music, for the next two hours we would praise in various ways however the Lord would direct us.

During those times back at our home church, the Spirit continued to guide us into deeper worship. One of the district leaders preached at our church one Sunday and told about a woman who wanted to sing a special song. She waved her hankies and said, "Got the devil by the tail on a downhill trod, yippee yew yea hippie yew yo." This got Sharon's attention. She has had an interest in prayer clothes and handkerchiefs for quite some time. She was impressed with Vestal Goodman's hankie. A point of contact is always a good, workable plan; this is what the hankie is for. Lace was sown on the first one. She loved it and wanted everyone to have one, so she bought hankies to have lace put on them.

God had other plans for these hankies. Instead of being something to cry into, they became something to minister to with. That is what Sharon has faithfully done even though it has not been easy. Much prayer by many people was required, and anointing oil was placed on them. Right away, some began to receiving healing and others got answers to prayers. Acts 19:12 KJV says that from Paul's body "were brought unto the sick handkerchiefs or aprons, and the diseases departed from them, and the evil spirits went out of them."

God gave Paul the power to do unusual miracles, so that even when his handkerchief or parts of his clothing were placed upon sick people, they were healed and any demons within them came out.

The woman with the issue of blood touched the hem of Jesus' garment. A minister visited a small, remote town to run a revival, and he stayed with some people who let him sleep in their bed. When he was leaving, the wife told the evangelist that her husband was not saved, and asked what she could do. He said, "Don't change the sheets." That night the husband woke up his wife and wanted to be saved. Who knows what God will do with these cloths since so many have prayed over them and anointed them? We have heard of many healings and deliverances.

I was asked to teach a class on the power of God. I am convinced He placed each student in that class to create a group that was called to pray as I taught on God's power and glory. It was awesome how God moved in that class as each of us experienced the presence and glory of God. Some later joined in the prayer group that started at home when we fasted and prayed. Later this same group met in other areas to pray, and the presence of the Lord was ever with us. After about eight years, I still experience the effects of that awesome time when God called us aside to praise and worship. These were times of seeking more of God and spending time with Him. I believe that as long as I am living according to His Word and doing all the things I should, the line is always open to heaven. I believe He will always be there to show me what I need to know. Why not try talking to Him one on one? When someone I talk with regularly calls me on the phone, I know by the voice who is calling. The Lord said, "My sheep know my voice."

CHANGE AND CHALLENGE

I believe these stories will help some of you to see how God is working with you.

There are times when God moves you out of your comfort zone to a place where you are not comfortable, as he did me several years ago. I was living in a cute townhouse near some friends and family when things happened that caused me to have to move to a small apartment away from all the things I had enjoyed. I am sure God was aware that I would adjust even though at the time I was not sure I could handle this move.

This was the beginning of a new walk with Him and new ways to minister. First, I stayed in my apartment most of the time praying. Most of my prayers were dedicated to giving in to God's will and at times asking Him to do what I willed. I was compelled to surrender to His will, and it was during this time that God began to take me to another level, which was very painful.

After retiring from my job, I began to sit before the Lord even more than I had before, which was many hours a day. Now it seemed He was requiring me to continue a search that I had started several years earlier. That search was in the deep recesses of my mind, day after day. I would not only search my thought life but I intensified my search for God's purpose for mankind and what He requires of us concerning His living Word. Most of us read, study, and know the letter of the Word, but what I was searching for was the spirit of the Word. The letter kills, but the spirit makes alive.

God's plans often bring changes to our plans, which can be very frustrating. Such change came to me, which was very disturbing because my lifestyle consisted of being with my great-grandchildren quite often, sharing a meal with a friend, receiving many visitors, and holding prayer groups in my home. That would all come to an end when I moved to a small apartment.

I found it is not easy to downsize so drastically while going through such radical change. Being a person who loves people, activities, and plenty of good scenery, pretty yards, and a good view, now I was in the last apartment on a hall that overlooked a large ditch, a railroad track, and dumpsters. There was no activity; no trees, birds, or people. And now there would be no more good times with my grandchildren and friends because we had to be considerate of the others living there whereas before I would run and play with them and laugh; now we had to be very quiet.

I was thinking at that point that God was not hearing my prayers or that Satan was out to destroy me. While I was trying to get settled, I began to experience some unpleasant things, and being in this state of mind caused more concern. I am convinced now that God was pressuring me to come close to Him and listen to Him, and that is just what I did.

It was a few nights after moving in that I sensed His presence in the room. It was early evening and I called on His name to direct me. He challenged me even more to return to the old path of faith and a new dedication, which led to a deeper relationship with Him. We can know Him and not have a real relationship with Him. I think of the ones here on earth that walked with Him and had a relationship with Him first. Of the twelve disciples, few were closer than Peter and James, but it was John who developed that intimate relationship with Him.

Before I had time to give it all to Jesus, I was leaving my apartment still perplexed, and feeling a need to go someplace more familiar. I was feeling very challenged and held out little hope of being able to serve God in this place as I had been accustomed to doing. Suddenly, a woman living in an apartment down the hall walked up and got right in my face, and I thought, "Oh my. What now?" I had talked to few people, but everyone seemed to know me. She began by saying, "Ruth Lee, you will never know what your presence here has done to this place. There is such change." I thought, "*What!* I have not done one thing." But I thanked her and went on my way confused about how I could possibly have done anything worthwhile the way I had been feeling.

Still, that was my first ray of hope that just maybe I could do some good for someone here. I began to look for ways I could bless the ones who had called me with unpleasant remarks. It has kept me from being upset or angry with them. The greatest help is when I can do something nice for them with love.

I learned that many years ago from one of my mentors. She had a bad experience with a pastor's wife. She was really upset and could not seem to forgive her. Even though she prayed and tried to forgive, her feelings soon turned into near bitterness. Then one day the pastor's wife called and asked if my friend could bake a cake for her because she had company coming and did not have time. Even though my friend wanted to forgive, she found it hard to do what the pastor's wife was asking her to do. As she prayed and complained a little, God spoke to her heart and said, "Bake her two cakes." She was even more frustrated, but as she thought about what God was asking of her, a forgiving spirit entered her heart and all the unforgiveness was gone. She baked the two cakes with joy.

If you are serious about seeking God's help, He will always meet your need. I learned many lessons from my predecessors, and one of them was to be understanding of people who say unpleasant, hurtful things to you. As I have traveled through life, I have said and done things that have hurt others, and when others do that to me, I have an understanding and forgiving heart because of my own imperfections. We are here to nurture and help one another through this life. God has given us experiences that will help us learn to do that. Even knowing we have done others wrong does not always make it easy to forgive. We must have God's help. We cannot do it on our own.

God will see us through. As 2 Timothy 1:9 KJV says, God "hath saved us, and called us with a holy calling, not according to our works, but according to his own purpose and grace, which was given us in Christ Jesus before the world began."

What we do in this life is a witness to others, the Word says. We are an open book read by all men. Our actions will be seen and be a pattern for others to live by, be it good or evil. Paul was sure of his walk and behavior, and he told others to follow him as he followed Christ. Other people are watching and following your life, especially members of your family. And if you do something, you cannot tell them they should not do it. Dads and moms must teach by example. If you want your children to have good lives and marriages, then they need to learn how by what you do as much or more than by what you say. Blessings and curses come by what you say and do.

In the early spring, while walking, I found myself focusing on angels. I realized I was to prepare a lesson on that subject. I began to research again, having taught on angels several times. But there is always more to learn, so I got my lesson together. Unhappy with my surroundings outside the building and with being at the end of the hall, I felt somewhat isolated.

I kept praying. I needed to recognize that God's plan for me was different from my plan, that I had no idea what He was doing in my ministry. I believe I was being led to surrender my will to His. I eventually abandoned my will to do what He had for me to do. About two years later, God gave me much more than I asked for or expected. It is obvious that it was His hand that did it.

It is the Spirit of God that makes the difference. God began to minister to me. I realized He was taking me to places where I had never been in Him. Soon He began to speak very plainly to me about many things, giving me words of wisdom and knowledge. My ministry to others began to intensify, with God helping me to know things I could not know within them.

I heard there was a Bible study on Wednesdays near my apartment, and if I was going to live there, that was the first thing I wanted to be involved in. I attended one and it went so well that I returned the next week. The lady leading the study was doing a good job teaching, and I did not plan to say anything unless I was called on by name. This could have been for two reasons—first so I would not be an intruder and second because I was pouting with God. The study was in Peter and the topic was angels, and I thought, "God, you are up to something, aren't you?"

At the end of the lesson, the teacher said, "I have never studied on angels. Have any of you?" I kept quiet because she was not addressing me personally, but then she said, "Ruth, do you know anything about angels?" I said I did because I had taught classes about them. She asked if I would teach on them in the next week or two.

That led to more time instructing. We would rotate, teaching about three months each. I had thought someone at another location would ask me to teach about angels, because God usually prepares me before

I am asked, but it was here He wanted me to teach. Though some are Baptist, Methodist, or Church of Christ and I am from a Pentecostal church and our church doctrines differ, the love of God bridges the gap. I respect their dedication and love for the Lord. It will be amazing when all of us get to heaven and find out it was the cleansing power of the blood of Jesus and His death on the cross that paved the road for everybody.

About a year later, when the Wednesday morning Bible study teacher retired, I was asked to take charge. The teacher had done a great job for quite some time, but she felt it was time for a change. As I began to teach, the Lord gave me a special love and concern for the people living in the apartment complex. Some are sick and do not drive, and so I wanted to provide a Sunday service for them. The first 3:00 p.m. church service was held on May 3, 2009. Some of the tenants' pastors from around the city had committed to come and minister, as did musicians and singers. God always has someone ready to do His work.

I believe this is the call to serve that I was feeling earlier. It always comes when you least expect it. I have tried to abandon my will to follow God's. That is what I call walking in His will, not knowing what tomorrow holds but being content to do whatever opens up for me. Not everyone understands that walk, but there is such contentment in walking in the Spirit and walking in His will.

This kind of life may not be for everyone, but if you have an interest in this type of prayer and if you are experiencing hard situations, you just might be one whom God is preparing for a special duty in His kingdom. Do not resist. Once you learn how to fight the enemy, it is a profitable thing. You will fight many battles as you learn, but God will always see you through them as He makes you stronger and more alert to the enemy.

Worship does not always come easy, nor is it always convenient, so you must make time for it. Intentional worship includes setting a time to pray. It can be any time of the day or night. I was working at my church, was involved in several ministries, and was really busy when I was moved to be more consistent in prayer. I allowed God to direct me. Soon I knew I was to set my clock for early in the morning. That could have been because I am at my best then. I set the alarm for 5:09 a.m. I was to be at work at 8:00, so that gave me almost two hours to worship, praise, pray, and sing. In one place where I lived, I had to be quiet, so I learned to do what was appropriate. Another place where I lived was very private. No one could hear my music, singing, and praying, so I really enjoyed my time with the Lord. But do not wait until everything is just right to start. Just begin and God will make things work out for you. I am retired now, though still very active, yet I still arise at a little after 5:00 with my heart turned to God from the time I get up. My methods change from time to time, but my program always includes worship, praise singing, prayer, and, of course, reading the Word.

COMPROMISE

The book of Romans lays a good foundation for a life free of compromise.

I beseech you therefore, brethren, by the mercies of God, that ye present your bodies a living sacrifice, holy, acceptable unto God, which is your reasonable service. And be not conformed to this world: but be ye transformed by the renewing of your mind, that ye may prove what is that good, and acceptable, and perfect, will of God. For I say, through the grace given unto me, to every man that is among you, not to think of himself more highly than he ought to think; but to think soberly, according as God hath dealt to every man the measure of faith … Be kindly affectioned one to another with brotherly love; in honour preferring one another; Not slothful in business; fervent in spirit; serving the Lord; Rejoicing in hope; patient in tribulation; continuing instant in prayer; Distributing to the necessity of saints; given to hospitality. Bless them which persecute you: bless, and curse not. Rejoice with them that do rejoice, and weep with them that weep. Be of the same mind one toward another. Mind not high things, but condescend to men of low estate. Be not wise in your own conceits. Recompense to no man evil for evil. Provide things honest in the sight of all men. If it be possible, as much as lieth in you, live peaceably with all men. Dearly beloved, avenge not yourselves, but rather give place unto wrath: for it is written, Vengeance is mine; I will repay, saith the Lord. Therefore if thine enemy hunger, feed him; if he thirst, give him drink: for in so doing thou shalt heap coals of fire on his head. Be not overcome of evil, but overcome evil with good. (Rom. 12:1–3, 10–21 KJV)

As you grow in the Lord and become a more mature believer, be aware of the tricks of the enemy. As he becomes more intense in striving for attention, I encourage you to keep growing! Be sure you are in obedience to God's Word. And always remember that if the Bible said something was a sin twenty years ago, it is still a sin today. Perhaps some ways we do things will change with time, such music, church buildings, and even methods of worship and praise, but the written Word is the same. And we must not seek to make it fit today's lifestyle.

Compromise is a dangerous thing. What I am about to say may seem harsh, but I ask you to prayerfully consider what follows. Many of today's young people are turned off by the anemic praise and worship that take place in many of today's congregations. They look around, asking themselves why they even come in the first place, and do not see any victory over depression, disease, divorce, or drugs. They listen to one or two hymns that may well have been vibrant when written but in so many cases have become nothing more than a weekly ritual. In short, Saul's weapons are not doing these fellowships any good. Why, then, should we be surprised that these future David's and Gideon's are turned off by them?

Leaders as well as regular Christians need to be honest before the Lord, listen to the Holy Spirit, and stop pretending. Because of compromise with sin and false gospels like easy believe-ism and legalism, many churches have become the comfortable nests for large numbers of very immature believers and varying numbers of tares. More mature, more spiritual believers are a minority and often feel out of place and not in tune with the fads and winds of doctrine that the very immature believers follow. If you are a mature believer, I encourage you to strive to keep growing in Him! Be sure you are in obedience to God's Word.

The Lord says,

> Ye shall know them by their fruits. Do men gather grapes of thorns, or figs of thistles? Even so every good tree bringeth forth good fruit; but a corrupt tree bringeth forth evil fruit. A good tree cannot bring forth evil fruit; neither can a corrupt tree bring forth good fruit. Every tree that bringeth not forth good fruit is hewn down, and cast into the fire. Wherefore by their fruits ye shall know them. Not everyone that saith unto me, Lord,

Lord, shall enter into the kingdom of heaven; but he that doeth the will of my Father, which is in heaven. Many will say to me in that day, Lord, Lord, have we not prophesied in thy name? And in thy name have cast out devils? And in thy name done many wonderful works? And then will I profess unto them, I never knew you: depart from me, ye that work iniquity. (Matt. 7:16–22 KJV)

And in Luke, we read,

Then said one unto him, Lord, are there few that be saved? And he said unto them, Strive to enter in at the strait gate: for many, I say unto you, will seek to enter in, and shall not be able. When once the master of the house is risen up, and hath shut to the door, and ye begin to stand without, and to knock at the door, saying, Lord, Lord, open unto us; and he shall answer and say unto you, I know you not whence ye are: Then shall ye begin to say, We have eaten and drunk in thy presence, and thou hast taught in our streets. But he shall say, I tell you, I know you not whence ye are [NIV: I do not know you or where you come from]; depart from me, all ye workers of iniquity. There shall be weeping and gnashing of teeth, when ye shall see Abraham, and Isaac. (Luke 13:23–28 KJV)

We often try to know a person by his performance, gifts, or personality, but James talks about walking the walk: "Be ye doers of the word and not hearers only." And Matthew 7 says, "It is not the one who says Lord, Lord that will enter in but he that doeth the will of the Father." I challenge you, therefore, to know the Word and obey it. Our eternal souls are not to be trifled with. This is the only chance we have to get it right.

THE POWER OF PRAISE AND WORSHIP

To some, praise might make a person look like he is in the flesh, but our emotions must be involved in praise whether it is singing, clapping, raising hands, or any other outward gesture. We are told to praise God in numerous ways. Praise the Lord! This is how the psalmist praised:

Praise God in his sanctuary;
Praise him in his mighty heavens!
Praise him for his mighty deeds;
Praise him according to his excellent greatness!
Praise him with trumpet sound;
Praise him with lute and harp!
Praise him with tambourine and dance;
Praise him with strings and pipe!
Praise him with sounding cymbals;
Praise him with loud clashing cymbals!
Let everything that has breath praise the Lord!
Praise the Lord!
—Ps. 150:1–6

As we consider God's greatness, we realize it is necessary to give Him praise. Praise can be a song, the clapping of hands, the raising of hands, or a dance. We should never compromise in praise by not praising as we should. When we are born again, we become aware of the awesome works of God in our lives, and then after we serve Him awhile, we see other reasons to praise Him. Then sometimes later on we cease to praise as we once did. Looking at Scripture, we find many examples of how throughout the Bible, the people of God have praised Him. We can praise God because He is powerful: "Accept our praise, O Lord, for all your glorious power. We will write songs to celebrate your mighty acts!" (Ps. 21:13 TLB). We can praise God for His goodness: "I will praise the Lord no matter what happens. I will constantly speak of His glories and grace. I will boast of all His kindness to me. Let all who are discouraged take heart. Praise God even when our heart is breaking." (Ps. 34:1–3 TLB).

The Bible says that God inhabits the praise of His people. *Inhabit* means to dwell in, live in, or abide in. God lives in our praise! We learn the principles of praise, but when the difficulties of life come and our hearts are breaking, it is easy to stop praising Him because we are hurting and praising Him is the furthest thing from our minds. However, the Holy Spirit prompts us to praise Him anyhow. At first, it feels out of place to praise Him when we are hurting and broken. But He deserves our praise for so many reasons.

The Bible says praising Him drives away discouragement and despair. All of a sudden, you discover that the negative feelings begin to disappear; your heart becomes glad, your whole mood and attitude change. Praising Him lifts you out of the pit; your eyes begin to see Him as the lifter of your head. Praising Him is doing spiritual warfare against the fiery darts the enemy hurls at you. There are benefits in praising Him! He pervades the spirit; His presence pushes aside pain and discouragement. So, no matter how bad you feel, praise Him! You will soon discover that praise is the way out of negative feelings and is the spiritual medicine for your soul.

Praise is a spiritual offering. "Through Jesus, therefore, let us continually offer to God a sacrifice of praise—the fruit of lips that confess His name" (Heb. 13:15 NIV). Praise is thanking God for His many gracious gifts. "Yes, I will bless the Lord and not forget the glorious things He does for me" (Ps. 103:2, TLB). Praise the Lord together and exalt His name, clapping your hands as you sing of His glory, raising your hands or saying *amen* to display your agreement with Him. These are some ways that we express praise.

In Revelation, we read,

> Then I saw a Lamb, looking as if it had been slain, standing in the center of the throne, encircled by the four living creatures and the elders.
>
> And they sang a new song: "You are worthy to take the scroll and to open its seals, because you were slain, and with your blood you purchased men for God from every tribe and language and people and nation. You have made them to be a kingdom and priests to serve our God, and they will reign on the earth." Then I looked and heard the voice of many angels, numbering thousands upon thousands, and ten thousand times ten thousand. They encircled the throne, the living creatures, and the elders. In a loud voice, they sang: "Worthy is the Lamb, who was slain, to receive power and wealth and wisdom and strength and honor and glory and praise!" (Rev. 5:6, 9–13 TLB)

WORSHIP

We must worship as well as praise God. Some view these, as the same, but I will endeavor to show the difference. First, praise is more of an outward emotion while worship is more of a heartfelt acknowledgment of Him in the spirit. The Bible tells us to worship God and Him only. When we worship, we enter into his Holy presence as we acknowledge who He is and recognize His power and awesomeness. Speaking to the Samaritan woman at the well, Jesus explained worship: "Yet a time is coming and has now come when the true worshipers will worship the Father in spirit and truth, for they are the kind of worshipers the Father seeks. God is spirit, and his worshipers must worship in spirit and in truth" (John 4:23–24).

The Complete Word Study Dictionary by Spiros Zodhiates, defines *worship* as *"proskuneo;* To worship, do obeisance, show respect, fall or prostate before. In the NT, generally, to do reverence or homage to someone, usually by kneeling or prostrating oneself before him ... Of God, used in an absolute sense ... with the words expressing prostration."

Sometimes we read a good verse in the Bible and somehow seem to forget it. It is so easy to try to find our worth in things and through people. I hope this verse makes you feel as special and important to God as it does me. "The Lord your God is with you. He is mighty to save. He will take great delight in you, He will quiet you with His love, He will rejoice over you with singing" (Zeph. 3:17 NIV).

> And the sound of a trumpet, and the voice of words; which *voice* they that heard intreated that the word should not be spoken to them any more: (For they could not endure that which was commanded, And if so much as a beast touch the mountain, it shall be stoned, or thrust through with a dart: And so terrible was the sight, *that* Moses said, I exceedingly fear and quake:) But ye are come unto mount Zion, and unto the city of the living God, the heavenly Jerusalem, and to an innumerable company of angels, To the general assembly and church of the firstborn, which are written in heaven, and to God the Judge of all, and to the spirits of just men made perfect, And to Jesus the mediator of the new covenant. (Heb. 12:19–24)

CHAPTER 5

TOTAL ABANDONMENT

"The eyes of the Lord move to and fro throughout the earth that He may strongly support those whose heart is completely His," 2 Chronicles 16:9 tells us. Many years ago, I heard these words: "It has not been seen what God can do with a man or woman who is fully surrendered to Him." I took the challenge and began a long journey toward abandonment of self. Now, more than thirty years later, I can see a notable change. However, I am not today what I used to be and I am not today what I will be. This is a great opportunity to start a more intensified journey toward a life of total abandonment. This is not done by taking one trip to an altar or making a one-time dedication. It takes time for God to change our thinking and motives. As He works on us and we continue our journey toward God, there will be much pleasure, much peace, and many benefits.

The word *abandonment* does not render the depth of the concept's meaning but gives us an idea how to surrender ourselves entirely to the guidance of the Holy Spirit. To abandon ourselves to God means that we must leave ourselves alone. We must take our hands off of ourselves and fall unconditionally into His hands. There comes a time—really many times—in the Christian walk when we know we must abandon ourselves to God. We know that we are being called out of our present place, spiritually and/or physically. We know we must go. But we have no clue as to where we are going. And we have no visible assurance that

God is with us. We must then choose. Will we play it safe and refuse to move, or will we abandon ourselves to God?

Christians throughout the ages, including missionaries, pastors, and lay people, have given their whole lives to Jesus. Yet so many others will never come close because they have their minds fixed on the things of this present world—making money and other self-serving pursuits. Others make an effort but never fully surrender, unwilling to forsake the pleasures of this life and inconsistent in the things of God. Talking to people, I've seen that the main problem is a resistance to giving their will and time to Jesus.

Some Old Testament men, such as Joseph, are a type of Christ, "choosing rather to suffer affliction with the people of God, than to enjoy the pleasures of sin for a season" (Heb. 11:25). As a child, Joseph might well have been taught by his mother the principles of God's kingdom. And we must learn them if we want to accomplish God's purpose in our lives. He said deny yourself, take up your cross, and follow me. In other words, when bad things are happening to you, rather than asking God to remove these trials, ask Him to see you through them. You will find that they won't hurt as much and the results will be of far more value. The sufferers will be the warriors.

We are being groomed for service to God. We may have to forgo the pleasures of life and be servants in undesirable situations to become God's special agents. We may not be part of the most popular groups. Sometimes, like Moses, we must travel to the back side of a barren region for a time to meet with God, learning His ways, rather than being up front with the elite in the palace of the king.

Paul chose to go bound to Jerusalem, knowing he might suffer death, rather than be part of the Sanhedrin crowd. He tells us how many times he was beaten and left for dead. He was let out of a window in a basket to escape his persecutors and endured many other sufferings and rejections to be prepared for some of the greatest ministries in the New Testament. He took up his cross to follow Jesus.

The path of faith isn't one merely leading to God's will. It is God's will. We often think that God's will is at the end of our journey. But it is not only at the end. The will of God is the journey itself.

The path of faith holds many obstacles, contradictions, and choices we must make to continue. As we overcome these, we grow. And yes, at the end of the journey we will receive the fullness of God's will—but only because along the way we became fit for it. Thus, by taking the way of faith, we do not merely receive a reward at the end. We do. But more importantly, we become something in Christ along the way—and this makes us able to receive. Thus, the path of faith not only leads to the will of God, but is the will of God!

The walk of faith is a journey in an uncertain direction, but we must trust the One leading us. In fact, as we travel the path of faith, it won't even seem like God is leading. It will seem like we are alone. Notice the word *seem*. What do we mean when we say it *seems* like God isn't with us? There comes a time in the Christian walk when the only reason we can give for believing God is with us is because He said He would be with us. We have no proof and we have no assurances we can see. We have only His promise. Abraham had such an experience. Notice the words of the writer of Hebrews concerning God's call to Abraham:

By faith Abraham, when he was called to go out into a place which he should after receive for an inheritance, obeyed; and he went out not knowing where he was going. By faith, he sojourned in the land of promise, as in a strange country, dwelling in tabernacles with Isaac and Jacob, the heirs with him of the same promise. For he looked for a city which hath foundations, whose builder and maker is God. (Heb. 11:8–10 KJV)

In Abraham's days, a person's entire future was wrapped up in physical inheritance. Lands were the primary source of wealth. To leave the place where your land was—land that had been in your family for generations—for a foreign land was a very real abandonment to God. Abraham was leaving everything behind, with nothing but a promise from God that he would receive a better inheritance.

Jesus' entire life was an abandonment of Himself to God. Perhaps the most profound expression of this abandonment is found in a statement He made upon the cross: "Father, into thy hands I commend my spirit" (Luke 23:46 KJV). In the Garden of Gethsemane, we also see total abandonment. He said, "Not my will, but thine, be done."

And we find Him combating the works of the devil, calling out demons as He was given power by God. There are those who enter a ministry, face normal problems, and succeed. Others struggle, facing lions, bears, and Goliaths, but this is all in God's plan to accomplish His will on earth.

A leap of faith is abandonment—not to where I think God is leading but to God Himself. I jump and fully trust that the One catching me will set me down where He wills.

You can work, worship, and do all the things I mentioned above without baptism in the Holy Spirit. However, this baptism makes you a better witness. It confers a power that is offered to all, and I highly recommend it. Some will never receive it, but we are still brothers and sisters in Christ Jesus and on our way to heaven if we are born again by the Spirit of God.

As the Scripture says, man looks at the outward appearance, but God looks at the heart. For example, a middle-aged lady who received Christ into her life, but knew nothing about how to pray or worship, began to watch and follow the main spiritual people in her church. She would set her clock an hour early to have time with God before leaving for work at 5:30. She developed crippling arthritis of the spine and was in much pain. Her doctor had told her she would soon be in a wheelchair and unable to walk. One day she called me and told me of her terrible pain and how she had to pick up her legs and put them in the car. She was not sure if she could work much longer. She asked if I could come over and take care of this. As we prayed, she confessed her healing. The years went by and she had not another complaint until she finally died in her mid-nineties of old age. She had been able to walk until the end.

In another case, I was amazed when God showed up in the life of a person who had only limited education and seemed to have no potential in this world or in God's kingdom. This person was struggling, making a mess of life, and not trying to get ahead in any manner until God entered and turned this soul around. Today this person serves God in seemingly impossible areas of ministry, and I would judge this person as being great in holy living and in God's service. These are the works of our God.

God is looking for people who will give Him their all. We must give our God both quality time and quietness. We must be willing to shut ourselves in with God and let all other voices be still. True, God speaks to us all day long. But when He desires to build something into our lives, His voice comes only after we have shut out every other voice.

Ask in faith. We do not obtain anything from God (including hearing His voice) unless we truly believe that He is able to convey His mind to us and enable us to understand His perfect will. Jesus says, "If a son shall ask bread of any of you that is a father, will he give him a stone? Or if he asks a fish, will he for a fish give him a serpent? Or if he shall ask an egg, will he offer him a scorpion?" (Luke 11:11–12 KJV). In other words, if you ask your heavenly Father for a word—a clear direction, a godly correction, a particular need—do you think for a moment He will instead let the devil come and deceive you?

The history of the church shows a host of men and women, such as Woodworth Etta, Smith Wigglesworth, and Watchman Nee, who have abandoned themselves and wholly followed Christ. Intercessors are a unique part of God's kingdom. As small children, we learn prayers for nighttime and before meals, such as "Now I lay me down to sleep." The new baby Christian prays very simple prayers that may not consist of more than "Jesus, I need you. Come and help me." When people are a little more mature in God, they begin to add more requests and venture into more congenial prayer, going on to intercession, which can be a more intense prayer, such as the one our Lord prayed in Gethsemane. We call these people prayer warriors. They stand in the gap for a friend, a family member, or the church. They are of great value.

Many books have been written on intercessory prayer and other kinds of prayer. Churches and pastors should feel free to call on intercessors to pray in certain situations that arise, not indulging all requests but praying for needs that will be borne up to God. There are some who have great compassion and make people feel good, while there are others oriented toward spiritual warfare.

God's kingdom has so many aspects to it, so many duties for people with different talents and callings. So there is no need for jealousies. If you find your place and help others with what they do, we will all accomplish more.

Prayer is required for any service to God, and yet prayer is not always all that is needed. It is important to know the Scripture so you will have good knowledge of the methods God uses when you are assigned to a task.

We must develop a faith in the One we serve, so we don't become discouraged while in training. We are often tempted to give up when conflicts arise. Training for God's special services, you sometimes wonder why you must suffer so much. Perhaps alone for long periods, you are at the mercy of God. There are no prayer partners or people with experience. It is just you and God. That is when you learn to accentuate the positive. Some may be trained under an experienced Christian, but others receive on-the-job training.

God doesn't always give us what we want. He gives us what we need. If we contend for what we want, He will sometimes honor our faith, only to our sorrow. It is best to trust Him to do what is best for us. The Bible counsels patience. Every new thing that we learn about God's Word is soon tested by experience, so we can be first partaker of the fruit, and then we can teach it not only from knowledge but from experience.

CHAPTER 6

EQUIPPING THE SAINTS

God did not leave us powerless; Jesus left us at least five potent tools. With any one of these, we can move mountains if we are trained by God or man to use them.

A soldier is never sent into battle without the proper equipment. I have found this ministry helps to be unfailing as long as I had the faith to put them into action and the ability to use it. As we enter into His service, we become more aware of God's provisions. I will describe five.

THE WORD

God's Word is both life and instruction; it brings life to all who will receive it. This book of instructions is inspired of God and is the Word of God. This living Word is quick and powerful and sharper than any sword, dividing asunder the soul and the spirit. The soul of man is where the old nature of Adam tries to rule and defeat us, keeping us from being obedient to God, trying to catch us off guard and throw us off balance. Try as we might, we cannot conquer the old man, so God left us His instructions. It is through the Scripture that we are empowered to be victorious over the flesh, or the old man.

"All Scripture is God-breathed and is useful for teaching, rebuking, correcting and training in righteousness," 2 Timothy 3:16–17 tells us.

The Scripture will help equip us for every good work. However, more is required of a workman. As 2 Timothy 2:15 says, "Do your best to present yourself to God as one approved, a workman who does not need to be ashamed and who correctly handles the word of truth."

How do we correctly handle God's Word? We must do more than just read and study it. James 1:22–26 explains the point rather well: "Do not merely listen to the Word, and so deceive yourselves. Do what it says. Anyone who listens to the Word but does not do what it says is like a man, who looks at his face in a mirror and, after looking at himself, goes away and immediately forgets what he looks like. But the man who looks intently into the perfect law that gives freedom, and continues to do this, not forgetting what he has heard, but doing it—he will be blessed in what he does. If anyone considers himself religious and yet does not keep a tight rein on his tongue, he deceives himself and his religion is worthless."

To read the Word and ignore it is foolish, and the person who does this has deceived himself. He is not truly following God. However, the man who reads the Word and does what it says will be blessed in all does, and the Word (the perfect law) will give him freedom. People who act religious but are deliberately not following the truth of God's Word are deceiving themselves. Their worship is not valid or accepted by God.

We learn in 1 Corinthians 2:10–13 that "The Spirit searches all things, even the deep things of God. For who among men knows the thoughts of a man except the man's spirit within him? In the same way, no one knows the thoughts of God except the Spirit of God. We have not received the spirit of the world but the Spirit who is from God, that we may understand what God has freely given us. This is what we speak, not in words taught us by human wisdom but in words taught by the Spirit, expressing spiritual truths in spiritual words."

THE NAME OF JESUS

What is so special about a name? In the old and new covenants, a name told what a person was or what he was like. The disciples James and John were called sons of thunder. Cephus was renamed Simon Peter. Jesus called him Peter, a rock. Lucifer lost his name, Morning Star. *Lucifer* is literally *the Shining One, Lightbringer,* or *Son of the Morning.* He became Satan, ruler of the darkness. Jacob was renamed Israel, a name of honor. Abram, a high father, became Abraham, the father of thousands.

The name of Jesus will never change. He will always be Savior. His name is higher and more powerful than any other. It can do wondrous things.

Do you cast out demons? If yes, thank God! If no, you have to understand that you too can drive out demons in the "name of Jesus" if you are a child of God, though only with great caution. These beings are very powerful. The only way a person can cast them out is when all his sins are forgiven and he is totally surrendered to God and acknowledges that it is His power at work. Our own power will never move them. When you know that God can and will act, you may begin exercising the authority that you have been given. Don't accept defeat. Rise up in faith. Stand on the Word of God and drive out the enemy. Receive the deliverance of the Lord. His name is a powerful one at which every knee will eventually bow. That name can do wonders to deliver us from the power of the enemy and the flesh. If you've been wringing you hands and worrying about what the devil is doing, it is time for you to put him under your feet. You have been given the power to use the name of Jesus, a name above every other. Jesus tells us, "Verily, verily, I say unto you, whatsoever ye shall ask the Father in my name, He will give it you."

The names Jesus and Emmanuel are synonymous. Why is Jesus the one who will save His people from their sins? Because He is Emmanuel, God with us. God became man. That's the reason for the Incarnation. The invisible God became a visible man. Talk about being with us. He could be seen, heard, touched, felt. And His touching us is the means by which the Almighty became a man. And the angel tells Joseph, that "you shall call His name Jesus, for He will save His people from their sins." He is the Savior.

The concept of name in Scripture involves much more than a tag that identifies a person and distinguishes him from other people. Although it does that, it also has a much deeper meaning. Name in Scripture represents the very essence of the person. A person's personality, character, reputation, and authority are all wrapped up in his name. Proverbs 22:1

says, "A good name is rather to be chosen than great riches." A good name is better than precious ointment.

It is scriptural to pray in the name of Jesus, as he Himself makes clear: "And whatsoever ye shall ask in my name, that will I do, that the Father may be glorified in the Son" (John 14:13, KJV)

THE BLOOD

The blood of Jesus has the power to cleanse us from sin; there is power in the blood to overcome sin in the flesh. When the blood is applied, sin is cleansed and forgiven. The blood of Jesus protects us and our houses. "And they overcame him by the blood of the Lamb, and by the word of their testimony; and they loved not their lives unto the death" (Rev. 12:11).

Hebrews says,

> Now when these things were thus ordained, the priests went always into the first tabernacle, accomplishing the service of God. But into the second went the high priest alone once every year, not without blood, which he offered for himself, and for the errors of the people: The Holy Spirit thus signifying that the way into the holiest of all was not yet made manifest ...But Christ being come an high priest of good things to come, by a greater and more perfect tabernacle, not made with hands, that is to say, not of this building; Neither by the blood of goats and calves, but by his own blood he entered in once into the holy place, having obtained eternal redemption for us. For if the blood of bulls and of goats, and the ashes of an heifer sprinkling the unclean, sanctifieth to the purifying of the flesh: How much more shall the blood of Christ, who through the eternal Spirit offered himself without spot to God, purge your conscience from dead works to serve the living God? ... And almost all things are by the law purged with blood; and without shedding of blood there is no remission of sins. (Heb. 9:6–8, 12–14, 22 KJV)

We overcome the enemy by the blood of the Lamb. We should have a bull-dog faith and never give up. "If thou hast run with the footmen, and they have wearied thee, then how canst thou contend with horses? and if in the land of peace, wherein thou trustedst, they wearied thee, then how wilt thou do in the swelling of Jordan?" asks Jeremiah 12:5.. We must plead the blood over our situation. We must watch the words that come out of our mouths. We cannot talk defeat and expect victory.

FAITH

Doctors all seem to think exercise is good for the body. It can help overcome many physical problems. Likewise faith is strengthened by exercise. If it is not used, it will not amount to much. The more you obey God's Word and put it into practice, the stronger your faith will be.

Faith believes in what is true. Faith has two elements: (1) being convinced of the truth, being certain of reality, and having evidence of unseen things; and (2) believing, hoping in, embracing, and seizing the truth.

Hebrews 11:1 says that "faith is the substance of things hoped for, the evidence of things not seen." While faith requires being convinced that what we believe in is true, just knowing the truth is only half of faith. God's word must be hoped for, embraced, seized! "The apostles said to the Lord, 'Increase our faith!' He replied, 'If you have faith as small as a mustard seed, you can say to this mulberry tree, "Be uprooted and planted in the sea," and it will obey you'" (Luke 17:5 NIV).

Believing is not exactly the same as faith. For belief to be faith, it must light on what is certainly true. Yet Scripture gives examples of situations where belief alone is required, even commanded. There's no time for evidence collection, for waiting, hearing, or certainty. Just believe. Like Peter walking on the water, we can't think. We must act! God requires us to believe in Him even when, temporarily, the evidence looks bad: to trust. God requires belief and trust in moments of human weakness, but faith is what makes us strong. Faith is the state of being convinced about what we hope for.

Contrary to popular teaching, faith is not mental delusion, presumption, or self-deception, but a work of the Holy Spirit and the Word of God. Faith comes by hearing the message, and the message is heard through the Word of Christ. .

THE HOLY SPIRIT

The Holy Spirit is in the world today to get a church ready for Christ's return. He gave us the Spirit so we could tread on serpents. This equips us with power to overcome anything that comes our way, and it equips the Special Forces with power to rush into a problem area and wipe out the pockets of evil spirits so the prayer warriors can wage war on the enemy.

Our spirit is where Jesus dwells by the Holy Spirit. When you accept Jesus, He kicks out Satan and takes up abode in our spirit. Then the blood of Jesus cleanses our souls from all unrighteousness. Now we are on our way to following God, and a fight begins that will last until we leave this life. Jesus said He casts out demons by the power of the Spirit of God. Jesus said, 'The Spirit of the Lord is upon me, because He has anointed me to preach the gospel to the poor … to set at liberty those who are oppressed" (Luke 4:18). "God anointed Jesus of Nazareth with the Holy Spirit and with power, who went about doing good and healing all who were oppressed by the devil, for God was with Him" (Acts 10:38).

The "ability" to cast out the demons comes from the power of the Holy Spirit. We know all the words to say and how to claim the promises, but we stand confused when nothing happens. James said if there is anyone sick, let him call for the elders of the church to anoint him with oil and the prayer of faith. You cannot have faith in God unless you are moving in God's realm. The way into God's realm is through repentance, confession, turning away from sin, and accepting Jesus, who moves in the Spirit. To get a church ready for Christ's return, God gave us the Spirit so we could tread on serpents.

We will never be able to use these five weapons without the authority from God to put them into effect. When Christ went away to heaven, he said, "Behold I give unto you power to tread on serpents and scorpions and nothing shall by any means harm you." Wow! What authority! But very few of us understand how to use this authority. To do this, we must move in the spiritual realm, where God is and where he tells us to move. That is the way to see the enemy flee and devils tremble. The name of Jesus will not send them fleeing unless you are in the Spirit.

Entering into the realm of the Spirit means more than praying and worshiping or feeling good. It involves entering into a place of God's knowledge, understanding what the enemy is like, and how you can defeat him. Sometimes you will feel a very quiet but strong urge to move against a situation you know is not natural or something you can handle.

It is by the authority given by God that we can speak the Word and it will work. So many times in the Bible, people spoke to situations and demons and they obeyed.

A certain slave girl possessed with a spirit of divination met Paul. "Paul, greatly annoyed, turned, and said to the spirit, 'I command you in the name of Jesus Christ to come out of her.' And he came out the very hour" (Acts 16:18 KJV).

Jesus spoke to the fig tree and it withered; He spoke to the storm and it ceased; He spoke to the cripple and he walked; He spoke to Lazereth and he came back to life. Peter said to the lame man, "Arise," and he was healed.

"For unclean spirits, crying out with a loud voice came out of many that were possessed: and many that were paralyzed and lame were healed" (Acts 8:7). The Bible says that you are the one who is supposed to overcome the enemy by the power of the Holy Spirit. Most of us do not like that kind of responsibility, but if we go with God, it is not that hard. Jesus spoke to the storm and the winds ceased. As it has been said, "Prayer is the key to heaven, but faith unlocks the door."

CHAPTER 7

THE POWERS OF HEAVEN AT YOUR DISPOSAL

"God hath spoken once; twice have I heard this that power belongeth unto God," says Psalm 62:11. Consider God's power in preservation. No creature has power to preserve itself. "Can the bush grow up without mire? Can the flag grow up without water?" (Job 8:11 KJV).

There are situations calling for new spiritual insight. "A multitude gathered from the surrounding cities to Jerusalem, bringing sick people and those who were tormented by unclean spirits, and they were all healed" (Acts 5:16). When you, like Caleb, feel you are ready to take that mountain full of giants, you can begin to do the works that Jesus did. This must take place in the Spirit. If you try through natural means, you will wind up like the seven sons of Sceva found in Acts:

> Some Jews who went around driving out evil spirits tried to invoke the name of the Lord Jesus over those who were demon-possessed. They would say, "In the name of Jesus, whom Paul preaches, I command you to come out." Seven sons of Sceva, a Jewish chief priest, were doing this. [One day] the evil spirit answered them, "Jesus I know, and I know about Paul, but who are you?" Then the man who had the evil spirit jumped on them and overpowered them all. He gave them such a beating

that they ran out of the house naked and bleeding. When this became known to the Jews and Greeks living in Ephesus, they were all seized with fear and the name of the Lord Jesus was held in high honor. Many of those who believed now came and openly confessed their evil deeds. A number who had practiced sorcery brought their scrolls together and burned them publicly. When they calculated the value of the scrolls, the total came to fifty thousand. In this way, the word of the Lord spread widely and grew in power. (Acts 19:13–20 NIV)

So if we are to command these spirits, we must know who we are in Christ and enabled by the Holy Spirit lest we become an example as these did.

Many people come to know Jesus, but not everyone will be chosen to serve on the front line. Consider Peter, James, and John, who are taken by Jesus into these more intimate situations. What are we being told by this circumstance? Not all of the disciples were ready for this. Or was it that God was training these three for a special work?

We must not waver about hearing His voice speak to our souls. Oh, we know that He speaks and that His sheep need to know the Master's voice. But in certain situations, doubts creep in and our ability to hear Him is weakened. We spend time "checking" the voice we heard, and when it is too big or too mysterious, we think, "This can't be God. Besides, the devil can speak, too. The flesh speaks; lying spirits speak. A multitude of voices come at us all the time. How can we know God's voice?" Three things are required of those who would hear God's voice:

1. An unshakable confidence that God wants to speak to you. You have to be fully persuaded that God longs to speak to you. Indeed, He is a speaking God and He wants you to know His voice so you can do His will. What God tells you will never go beyond the boundaries of Scripture. And you don't have to have a Ph.D. to understand His voice. All you need is a heart that says, "I believe God desires to talk to me."

2. Quality time and quietness. You need to be willing to shut yourself in with God and let all other voices be still. True, God speaks to us all day long. But whenever He has wanted to build something into my life, His voice has come only after I have shut out every other voice but His.

3. Ask in faith. We do not obtain anything from God (including hearing His voice) unless we truly believe that He is able to convey His mind to us and to enable us to understand His perfect will.

David Wilkerson wrote, "Those who truly know God have learned how to recognize his voice above all others. He wants you to be absolutely convinced that he desires to talk to you and tell you things you've never seen or heard before."

CHAPTER 8

THE BATTLE IS NOT YOURS

Even though we know all the words, phrases, and how to claim the promises verbally, we stand confused when nothing happens. We must return and ask God to lead us and give us wisdom to accomplish His work, and as we do that, we will be amazed at how the Word works. There is a place for everyone. You could be a new Christian or unlearned in the Word, but if you are acting in the Spirit realm and on your faith, it will work. We should all function in these areas. You don't have to be specially trained for this. It is in strategic areas that we need the more trained warhorses. Some of us can move alongside like the other part of David's army.

God needs special agents who are willing to fight in battles against our fierce enemies, willing to be trained to move in the Spirit for the battle, learning what it means when He said, "We wrestle not against flesh and blood, but against principalities, powers, darkness and wickedness." When we defeat them, the battle is won. And we must not take God lightly. When we disobey His word, we should not think He will always pour out His blessings on us. Remember Samson.

We use the name of Jesus and quote Scriptures, and we are disappointed because God does not do what we asked. One reason we don't receive what we want is that in God's kingdom the ways of accomplishing His will are opposite the natural ways we do things here on earth. Many times we try to use this world's methods when they do not work in the spiritual world. When we live in the natural world, we will always be looking for things to satisfy the flesh—all kinds of entertainment, vacations to get away. But God is so satisfying to the spiritual man that he will have much less need for the natural, only what is necessary for the body to rest and be refreshed. The soul finds its rest in Him. So many are dissatisfied because they have advanced to this type of living. Many will never enter into this Promised Land because of unbelief. While it is not likely to keep you out of heaven, it will keep you from having peace and contentment and from accomplishing all you could for God. Some find this kind of rest in a hard day of labor for the Lord, some in prayer, some in serving others; the natural man finds his in getting away from everything. We live in a do-it-yourself world. We think we must learn the normal tricks of the trade to be successful in the Lord's work. The Bible way is to love those who hate you. Giving is the way to obtaining. Go the second mile.

This is the righteousness that is only through Jesus Christ. Without righteousness, we will never be able to fight the battle. We cannot influence others and win souls to Christ unless we are what we claim to be. We must have our feet shod with the gospel of peace.

The good fight of faith means never, never giving up. God is omniscient. He knows the plan of the enemy and has provided special revelation for us that we might be informed to protect ourselves from Satan's attacks through the full armor that comes to us in Christ.

In the book of Joshua, we see the dramatic, unexpected appearance of a mysterious man with a drawn sword in combat readiness. Joshua immediately asked him, "Are you for us or for our adversaries?" Joshua had been waiting forty years; he was ready to fight. Joshua asked the wrong question. The man replied, "No; rather I indeed come now as captain of the host of the Lord." How often do we go to God asking the wrong questions?

Who was this "captain of the host of the Lord"? A "host" in the Bible is an unseen army, invisible to the human eye, that surrounds the throne of God. It is an angelic host. Christ said twelve legions of angels were ready to defend Him. Joshua immediately recognized the supernatural character of this visitor. Joshua was in the presence of God. "And Joshua fell on his face to the earth, and bowed down, and said to him, 'What has my lord to say to his servant?'" Joshua fell on his face and worshiped. The worship paid to this messenger of the Lord is directed to Yahweh Himself. Who is this person?

It is sin to worship angels and men. The passage indicates that a superhuman person is present. He is in the presence of deity. The commander of the army of the Lord is God Himself. Yahweh has come to lead and fight for His people. All distinctions between the messenger of the covenant and the Lord Himself evaporate. Joshua 5:15 removes any doubt as to who this "captain of the army of Yahweh" was. "The captain of the Lord's host said to Joshua, 'Remove your sandals from your feet, for the place where you are standing is holy.' And Joshua did so." In the Bible, things, places and people can be called holy only because they are set aside for God or claimed by Him.

When things get dangerous for us, it is important to see that the battle is not ours. This is a great example of how God will always be there when we need him. We must build up bulwarks for our children and the generations to come, set up landmarks to say, "This is the way; walk ye in it." The time is at hand when people will not receive sound doctrine. We must proclaim it in the face of all opposition.

"So Judah gathered together to seek help from the Lord; they even came from all the cities of Judah to seek the Lord. Then Jehoshaphat stood in the assembly of Judah and Jerusalem, in the house of the Lord before the new court, and he said, 'O Lord, the God of our fathers, are You not God in the heavens? And are You not ruler over all the kingdoms of the nations? Power and might are in Your hand so that no one can stand against You'" (2 Chron. 20:4–6 KJV).

Sometimes, if we are to win victory, the Lord has to be the One to fight the battle. This is the way it must be to prevail over sins. Only through what God has done can we gain the victory. We cannot redeem ourselves from our sins. We have no price to offer. That battle must be the Lord's! There are many examples of this principle throughout the pages of Scripture. An alliance of Moab, Ammon and others had invaded Judah. It was a matter of mathematics. The enemy by far outnumbered the people of Judah. There seemed to be only one possible outcome: the defeat of Judah.

Jumping up, Jehoshaphat stood in the temple and prayed. There was only one place to turn. Sometimes life is like that. And with reference to death and eternity, God is the only One who can make a difference!

The Lord responded through His prophet, Jahaziel. "And he said, 'Listen, all Judah and the inhabitants of Jerusalem and King Jehoshaphat: thus says the Lord to you, "Do not fear or be dismayed because of this great multitude, [or your many problems] for the battle is not yours but God's."'" (2 Chron. 20:15).

Yes, here was a case where the battle had to be the Lord's, or it would be lost. However, that the battle was the Lord's did not mean that the people of Judah were to sit and do nothing. They were instructed: "You need not fight in this battle; station yourselves, stand and see the salvation of the Lord on your behalf, O Judah and Jerusalem. Do not fear or be dismayed; tomorrow go out to face them, for the Lord is with you." (2 Chron. 20:17). They went out and faced their enemy, and the Lord gave them victory as they watched the enemy's alliance fall apart and the former allies attack one another. Because the battle is not yours does not mean you sit down and do nothing. Rather it means that when you fight, God will direct the battle and bring the victory.

"Get yourself up on a high mountain, O Zion, bearer of good news, Lift up your voice mightily, O Jerusalem, bearer of good news; Lift it up, do not fear. Say to the cities of Judah, 'Here is your God!' Behold, the Lord God will come with might, With His arm ruling for Him. Behold, His reward is with Him and His recompense before Him. Like a shepherd He will tend His flock, In His arm He will gather the lambs and carry them in His bosom; He will gently lead the nursing ewes" (Isa. 40:9–11).

This is what is known as a messianic prophecy because it speaks of events having to do with the coming of the Messiah, all of which were fulfilled with the incarnation of the Word of God, Jesus of Nazareth, some seven centuries later. One cannot help but think of Jesus as these verses are read. Isaiah is talking about "good news" and in fact, the word *gospel* as in "the gospel of Jesus Christ" means *good news*. God sent His Son to be the redeemer of the world. Without God, there would be no Savior. As human beings, we sometimes wonder what God is like; let us now take a look at how God makes Himself known.

God is no longer "no longer" and will not be for the rest of eternity a hidden, invisible God. He has revealed Himself through His Son.

The Hubble Telescope has given us a hint of God's awesome creation. He tells us to consider the works of His hands. No one can begin to explain all that He has made. He has given us a record of some of His creation that pertains to us here on earth. Yet with our finite minds, even the Word is sometimes hard to comprehend.

We can see that there is perfect origination in the kingdom of God; the entire body of the Word sets forth a well-organized kingdom with principalities, powers, ministering spirits, and perhaps other unknown sources of provision for us and other beings. These forces stand in their place to move only at His command. Heaven is a highly organized place. We can look at our government and get a dim view of how heaven functions. The Father gave the plan to man to organize our government. It is seemingly set up after the pattern of heaven.

Things seen are made after things not seen. From the beginning of the written Word, we see God, who is the head of everything, setting forth the plural name *Elohim* to show the Trinity. Even in the Trinity, we find there is a chain of command. God the Father is in charge, Jesus was sent by the Father, and so was the Spirit. In teaching the disciples to pray, Jesus said, "Say our Father which art in heaven." Later, He invited to "ask anything in my name." I do not see how anybody could go wrong by praying to the Father in Jesus' name. Jesus accepts worship, but even He directed His prayers to the Father and gave us a pattern prayer to do the same.

The Holy Spirit seems to give all praise and adoration to God the Father and His Christ, and that promised Holy Spirit is the guarantee of my inheritance until I acquire the possession of it (Eph. 1:13–14 ESV). As humans, we seem to find it hard to follow that chain of command. Some even try to tell angels what to do. And that seems a little off balance to me. God sends forth his holy angels to do His work; they seem to bring the answers that God gives, as in Daniel. When things get dangerous for us, it is important to see this truth and know the battle is not ours.

Throughout His word, we find how God has placed each of His created beings in a certain place to do an assigned duty. We also see that member of the Trinity has own duties. The Father is head of all things. He is the creator, redeemer, and covenant-keeper. Jesus is our high priest and savior, and the Holy Spirit is the sent one, the power of the kingdom. The three are in complete agreement in everything. The church and the home are planned by God. The Father is the head of the Trinity. Christ is the head of the church. Man is the head of his home (1 Cor. 11: 3 KJV). But the head of every man is Christ, the head of the woman is the man, and the head of Christ *is* God. Christ took His place and is now seated on the right hand of God. The Holy Spirit is in His place with mankind here on the earth, sent by God to be the power of God in the church, to lead and guide us into truth.

Jesus called His twelve disciples to Him; He gave them power over unclean spirits, to cast them out, and to heal all kinds of sickness and disease. But Paul vehemently rejected any kind of worship. God has placed man in charge of His work here on earth. Jesus said, "And as you go, preach, saying, 'The Kingdom of heaven is at hand … cast out demons" (Matt 10:7, 8). Jesus said, "All authority has been given to Me in heaven and on earth" (Matt 28:18). He not only gave it to the seventy He sent out and the ones He had trained, but Scriptures tell us clearly that Jesus gave His disciples "power" over the enemy. "Behold, I give you the authority to trample on serpents and scorpions, and over all the power of the enemy and nothing shall be any means hurt you" (Luke 10:19). Though we have authority, no one prays to us.

But not all seem to have the power He gave. Does the secret lie in <u>those who believe?</u> "And these signs will follow those who believe: In My name they will cast out demons; they will speak with new tongues" (Mark 16:17). Jesus is our friend, redeemer, and guide. He is worthy of our praise..

"And I will ask the Father, and he will give you another advocate to help you and be with you forever—the Spirit of truth. The world cannot accept him, because it neither sees him nor knows him. But you know him, for he lives with you and will be in you" (John 14:16–17 NIV).

The Holy Spirit teaches us to pray and leads us into worship. He guides into all truth. "In the same way the Spirit also helps our weakness; for we do not know how to pray as we should, but the Spirit Himself intercedes for us with groaning too deep for words" (Rom. 8:26 KJV). In John

14:26, Jesus says, "But the Helper, the Holy Spirit, whom the Father will send in My name, He will teach you all things, and bring to your remembrance all that I said to you." In John 15:26, he says, "When the Helper comes, whom I will send to you from the Father, that is the Spirit of truth who proceeds from the Father, He will testify of me."

We must be saved and therefore receive the Spirit that will help us spiritually discern the truth of God's Word. Then we must do what it says. "We know that we have come to know him if we obey his commands. The man who says, 'I know him,' but does not do what he commands is a liar, and the truth is not in him. But if anyone obeys his word, God's love is truly made complete in him" (1 John 2–5).

This is how we know we are in Him: There may be times when we decide to physically react to the Lord as we worship Him. We may want to praise Him and show him honor in physical ways, perhaps falling face down before Him as we earnestly pray for a request. To worship means to show honor, respect, and the superiority of the one you are worshiping. True worship will draw attention to the one we are honoring, not to ourselves. We do that best by living a life each and every day that is holy and pleasing to the Lord.

In Matthew 28:16–20, Jesus gave us the great commission to go into all the world. This includes preaching and teaching the Word and making disciples of all. In Genesis, the Word tells us that the earth has been given to mankind and that as believers we are to subdue it for the glory of God.

As we come to the close of this book, let us all remember to live by the Good Book, believe what it says, and act on its promises by faith, and may the God of all grace preserve us all until that great day.

When preparing for a special occasion, we want to dress appropriately. This world is our dressing room as we get ready for our eternal home. It seems to take us a lifetime to put off all the wrong things, get cleaned up, and dressed in the right things. Colossians talks about putting off lying, cheating, and evil speaking and putting on the new man. We are on a journey. We are here only for a while, so it is imperative for us to do all we can while we can. Most everyone is interested in prizes and rewards. God has set up a plan, and what we do here on earth will merit us a reward, whether it be good or evil. So what we do now will determine what our reward will be at the judgment. May the Lord God of all grace keep your heart and mind until that day.

"Now unto him that is able to do exceeding abundantly above all that we ask or think, according to the power that worketh in us. Unto him be glory in the church by Christ Jesus throughout all ages, world without end. Amen" (Eph. 3:20 KJV).

This life is full of suffering, and we may languish over problems. As Psalm 34:19 says, "Many are the afflictions of the righteous, but the Lord delivers him out of them all." But the way of the transgressor is hard, and he does not have the help of God as the believer does.

If you would like to know Him today, say this prayer with me.

God of all grace, I know I am a sinner. I come to you asking you to forgive me of all of my sins. I believe you came to this earth, died on the cross for my sins, were raised from the dead, and now sit at the right hand of God, forever interceding for your people.

I accept your forgiveness for my sins and receive you now as my personal savior.

Name_____

Date_____

You who have prayed this prayer must now read your Bible every day and pray to God in Jesus' name. Then you must find a good, Bible-believing Protestant church that will help you mature in Christ. May the Lord bless you and meet your needs daily. Allow Him to use you to help others know Jesus Christ.

Allow this book to show you how to depend on God. For more information on how to live for the Lord, you may write me at 285 Sylvest Drive, Apt. 214, Montgomery, AL 36117 for material that will help you get started.

Acknowledgments

I wish to thank the following people for their inspiration, knowledge, and other help in creating this book:

Shirley Ingram, who inspired me and encouraged me to write this book.

Wendy Bedsole and Debbie Blankenship, who spent countless hours editing and proofing.

Professor Becky Jacobson, who spent hours proofing and made valuable suggestions.

The Rev. Johnny Jones, who read the rough draft and checked for theological errors.

Steve Sweeney, who offered encouragement in many ways.

Kim Astorga, who helped with proofing and encouragement.

The following sources offered invaluable information:

Bill Burns, *THE TRUMPET, His Kingdom Prophecy,* April 26, 2010)

David Wilkerson, *Recognizing God's Voice,* Time Square Church, New York City..

Bible translations cited include the *King James Version* (KJV), the *New International Version* (NIV), and *The Living Bible* (TLB).

ABOUT THE AUTHOR

Ruth Lee, author of *Straight Paths to the Supernatural,* challenges people to pray. She is an avid student of God's word and a constant prayer warrior. Her walk with God has been steady and unwavering for forty-nine years.

Ruth was born into a Christian home in 1930 near Pittsburgh, Pennsylvania. She was brought up in the fear and admonition of the Lord by her parents, who were evangelists. Her dad's ancestors from the seventeen hundreds on had been pastors, deacons, and leaders in the church. These heads of homes guided their families in a godly manner. Ruth was consistently taught the Bible during her formative years. Her adult interests have been in the study of the kingdom of God and the kingdom of Satan.

She was married to Hubert Lee and is the mother of two daughters, Deborah and Laura. She has three grandchildren and seven great-grandchildren. Her husband went to his eternal reward in 1994. They were married for 45 years.

Ruth was licensed with the Assemblies of God in 1982. She ministered for seven years on Christian television, producing and hosting a variety show touching on subjects pertinent to Christian and secular life. Most of her other ministry has been to adults, teaching them about godly living, eternal life, and the dangers of an ungodly life. She trained teachers for seven years. Her studies have taken her through the Old Testament about thirty times and the New Testament nearly a hundred times. Though she is eighty-two and has studied, taught, and ministered for forty-nine years, she has not retired. She is the coordinator of the sharing and caring ministries at her home church, leads a church service every Sunday afternoon for residents of a retirement home, and conducts a Wednesday morning Bible study. Always dedicated to God, Ruth endeavors to share what she has learned with those she meets and to lead as many as possible to the saving knowledge of Jesus Christ. While acknowledging she is not perfect, she is confident that she will be made perfect by our Lord and Savior on that final day. Her goal is to stand before Christ and have Him say, "Well done, my good and faithful servant."